CCE-CRA

Comptroller of the Currency
Administrator of National Banks

Community Reinvestment Act Examination Procedures

Comptroller's Handbook

October 1997

Revised for Web publication
May 1999

CCE

Consumer Compliance Examination

Community Reinvestment Act
Examination Procedures

Table of Contents

Community Reinvestment Act
Examination Procedures

Introduction

The Community Reinvestment Act examination procedures for small banks appear in a separate booklet, "Community Bank Consumer Compliance Examination Procedures."

Background and Summary

The Community Reinvestment Act (CRA) of 1977 (12 USC 2901), as amended, encourages each insured depository institution covered by the act to help meet the credit needs of the communities in which it operates. The CRA requires that each federal financial supervisory agency assess the record of each covered depository institution in helping to meet the credit needs of its entire community, including low- and moderate-income neighborhoods, consistent with safe and sound operations, and take that record into account when deciding whether to approve an application by the institution for a deposit facility.

Neither the CRA nor its implementing regulations inject hard and fast rules or ratios into the examination or application processes. Rather, the law contemplates an evaluation of each lender's record that can accommodate individual circumstances. Neither the CRA nor its implementing regulations require financial institutions to make high risk loans that jeopardize their safety. To the contrary, the law makes it clear that lending that meets an institution's CRA responsibilities should be done within the bounds of safety and soundness. Rebuilding and revitalizing communities through sound lending and good business judgment should benefit both the communities and financial institutions.

An institution's capacity to help meet community credit needs is influenced by many factors, including its financial condition and size, resource constraints, legal impediments, and local economic conditions that could affect the demand and supply of credit. Examiners must consider these factors when evaluating an institution's performance under CRA. This is consistent with a fundamental underpinning of the CRA regulations — that the differences in institutions and the communities in which they do business preclude rigid rules. The CRA regulations and procedures contain clear, flexible, and sensible performance criteria that accommodate differences in institutions and their communities, minimize burden, promote consistency and objectivity, and allow examiners to be guided by common sense rather than adherence to mechanistic procedures.

For example, the CRA regulations provide for different evaluation methods to respond to basic differences in institutions' structures and operations. The regulations provide a streamlined assessment method for small institutions that emphasizes lending performance; an assessment method for large, retail banks that focuses on lending, investment, and service performance; and an assessment method for wholesale and limited-purpose institutions based on community development activities. Further, the regulations also give any institution, regardless of size or business strategy, the choice to be evaluated under a strategic plan. This type of flexibility and customizing should permit institutions to be evaluated fairly and in conformance with their business approach.

Examination Burden Reduction

The complementary regulatory themes of flexibility, responsiveness, and objectivity are extended to the examination process as part of an overarching effort, among other things, to reduce the burden of the regulations and the examination on institutions. Indeed, both the regulations and the examination procedures reflect a conscientious effort to minimize burden on financial institutions. For example, examiners are encouraged to draw on the results of previous examinations of an institution for information about major product lines, business strategy, and supervisory restrictions. This information is typically available from agency sources and can often be reviewed off-site. Further, examiners may already have knowledge of an institution's community and local demographics from their own past visits to the institution or to others in the same area. In these cases, examiners should be able to develop a good understanding of the context in which an institution operates before the actual examination begins, and then just supplement and update that understanding upon arrival at the institution.

The regulations focus on performance-based criteria, not process or documentation. Institutions are not to be evaluated on how well they ascertain community credit needs, how energetically they market and advertise their products, or how actively members of their boards of directors participate in local community organizations or civic groups. Consequently, the paperwork burden long associated by institutions with these past evaluation factors has been eliminated, as has any consideration of these factors from the examination process.

This sets the stage for a more constructive, credible, efficient, and unobtrusive examination process that concentrates on results. Both the regulations and the examination procedures promote and establish evaluation methods based on reviewing objective data that institutions can also use to measure their own performance. This should further minimize burden since examination results will be more understandable and, over time, more predictable.

Rather than a "one-size-fits-all" examination, separate procedures have been developed for small and large banks, as well as for those that are wholesale or limited purpose, and those that are operating under an approved strategic plan. Further, examiners are expected to use common sense to tailor the examination to mitigate the burden on the institution; for example, they can perform some procedures in advance of the on-site examination. This tailoring allows examiners to take reasonable steps to reduce burden while ensuring that the examination process is more understandable for the institution.

Performance Context

An institution's performance under the regulatory assessment criteria is evaluated in the context of information about the institution, its community, and its competitors. The examiner will review demographic and economic data about the institution's assessment area(s) and information about local economic conditions, the institution's major business products and strategies, and its financial condition, capacity, and ability to lend or invest in its community. Often, this review will be facilitated by gathering information from examinations of other institutions serving the same or similar assessment areas, reviewing information from other recent community contacts, and reviewing information about the assessment area developed cooperatively by the different agencies.

The examiner will also review information an institution chooses to provide about lending, investment, and service opportunities in its assessment area(s). The examiner will not, however, require the institution to create such information, nor will the examiner ask for any information other than what the institution may already have developed as part of its normal business practice. An examiner should not evaluate an institution on its efforts to ascertain community credit needs, market its products, geocode its loans, or record CRA-related discussions in its board minutes nor rate an institution on the quality of any contextual information that it may provide.

Role of Community Contacts

Interviews with local community, civic, or government leaders can help examiners learn about the community, its economic base, and local community development initiatives. They can also help examiners understand public perceptions of how well local institutions are responding to credit needs. These interviews help provide balance to the examiner's understanding of the performance context. Community contact interviews normally take the form of personal meetings, but telephone conversations or larger group meetings may also be appropriate.

Information from community contacts can provide valuable insights to examiners, particularly to those who have relatively little experience or familiarity with an institution's assessment area. Contacts may be made as part of an examination, or before the start of an examination, and typically will be conducted by the examiners responsible for the CRA examination. Wherever possible, however, the agencies will draw on recent local interviews conducted by other agency staff, or by other regulatory agencies with CRA responsibilities. (See "Community Contact Procedures" on page 9 for additional information.)

Assessment Area Considerations

Institutions are required to identify one or more assessment areas within which the agencies will evaluate the institution's performance. In most cases, an institution's assessment area will be the town, municipality, county, some other political subdivision, or the MSA in which its branches are located and a substantial portion of its loans are made. If an institution chooses, however, its assessment area need not coincide with the boundaries of one or more political subdivisions (e.g., counties, cities, and towns or MSAs), so long as the adjustments to those boundaries reflect the fact that the institution's assessment area(s) would otherwise be too large for the institution to serve, have an unusual configuration, or would include significant geographic barriers. When the assessment area coincides with recognized political subdivisions, or has not changed in any way since the previous examination, examiners may not have to conduct a comprehensive reevaluation of the assessment area.

When evaluating an institution's performance, the examiner will use the assessment area designated by an institution provided that it meets regulatory criteria. Only if the criteria have not been satisfied will the examiner revise the assessment area so that it complies with the regulations. The revisions will be discussed with institution management, and the revised assessment area will be used to evaluate performance. Unless the assessment area reflects illegal discrimination, however, examiners will not consider problems with the designation of the assessment area when assigning a rating to the institution. Consequently, burden associated with the delineation of communities and inconsistencies resulting from examiners criticizing community delineations as being too large at one examination and too small at the next should be eliminated.

Large Bank Performance Criteria

The large bank performance criteria — the lending, investment, and service tests — cover all banks with assets of $250 million or more and banks, regardless of asset size, owned by holding companies with total bank and thrift assets of $1 billion or more unless they requested designation and received approval as wholesale or limited-purpose institutions or have been approved for evaluation under a strategic plan.

Examiners are expected to exercise judgment and common sense to minimize the burden imposed by the examination process, consistent with a complete and accurate assessment of performance. For example, examiners may be able to use economic and demographic data analyzed in an examination of one bank in examinations of other institutions serving the same or similar assessment areas. Community contacts may also be combined to cover more than one institution in a given market. In cases where an institution has analyzed its CRA performance, examiners may use those analyses, after verifying their accuracy and reliability, and should supplement those analyses only where questions are raised. Examiners should consider any performance-related information offered by an institution but should not request information not called for by examination procedures.

Large banks face burdens that small banks do not, particularly in data collection and reporting. Using automated data from large banks, examiners should be able conduct much of the necessary analysis before traveling to the examination site. Doing so should reduce any disruptions caused by the presence of examiners at the bank. Examiners must be sensitive to the burden of the examination process and use judgment and common sense when conducting examinations, performing only those steps necessary to arrive at an accurate assessment of the bank's performance.

Wholesale/Limited-Purpose Performance Criteria

In order to be evaluated under the community development test, an institution must be designated as a wholesale or limited-purpose institution following submission of a written request to its primary regulator. Once an institution has received a designation, it will not normally have to reapply for that designation. The designation will remain in effect until the institution requests that it be revoked or until one year after the agency determines that the institution no longer satisfies the criteria for designation and notifies the institution of this determination.

Wholesale or limited-purpose institutions are evaluated on the basis of their:

- Community development lending, qualified investments, or community development services.

- Use of innovative or complex qualified investments, community development loans, or community development services and the extent to which investments are not routinely provided by private investors.

- Responsiveness to community credit and development needs.

Examiners must be cognizant of the context within which a wholesale or limited-purpose institution operates. Examiners should recognize that these institutions may tailor their community development activities based on their own circumstances and the community development opportunities available to them in their assessment areas or the broader statewide or regional areas that include the assessment areas.

Institutions need not engage in all three categories of community development activities to be considered "satisfactory" under the community development test. Community development loans, investments, and services can be directed to a statewide or regional market that includes the institution's assessment area and still qualify for consideration under the community development test as benefitting the assessment area. Moreover, if an institution has a satisfactory community development record in its assessment area, all community development activities regardless of their locations should be considered.

Like other performance tests, community development tests should employ only those analyses that are necessary to reach an accurate conclusion about the institution's performance, should use all available, reliable information, and should avoid duplication of effort to reduce burden.

Strategic Plans

The regulations permit any institution to develop, and submit for approval by its primary supervisory agency, a strategic plan for addressing its responsibilities with respect to CRA. The regulations require that the plan be developed in consultation with members of the public and that it be published for public comment. The plan must contain measurable annual goals. A single plan can contain goals designed to achieve only a "satisfactory" rating or, at the institution's option, can contain goals designed to achieve a "satisfactory" rating, as well as goals designed to achieve an "outstanding" rating.

This approach to addressing an institution's CRA responsibilities presents an opportunity for a very straightforward examination. The first question an examiner should investigate is whether the goals were met. If they were, the appropriate rating should be assigned. The appropriateness of the goals will have already been determined in the process of public comment and agency review and approval. Consequently, further investigation relating to the context of the institution should not be necessary. Obviously, if some or all of the plan's goals were not met, the examiner will be required to evaluate such issues as whether they were substantially met and in doing so will have to exercise some judgment regarding the degree to which they are missed and the causes.

The examiner, however, should approach an examination of an institution operating under a plan understanding that part of the purpose for these regulatory provisions was to give the institution significant latitude in designing a program that is appropriate to its own capabilities, business strategies, and organizational framework as well as to the communities that it serves. Consequently, the institution may develop plans for a single assessment area that it serves, for some, but not all, of the assessment areas that it serves, or for all of them. It may develop a plan that incorporates and coordinates the activities of various affiliates. It will be the examiner's challenge to evaluate institutions operating under one plan or a number of plans in a way that accurately reflects the results achieved and that sensibly wraps that evaluation into the overall assessment of the institution.

As with other aspects of the CRA examination, the examiner should first make the greatest use possible of information available from the agencies to evaluate performance under the plan. It is likely, however, that some elements of a plan under review will not be reflected in public or other agency data. Consequently, the examiner may, of necessity, have to ask the institution for the data necessary to determine whether it has met its goals. The examiner should do so, to the greatest extent possible, by asking the institution to provide data for review before going on-site for the examination. The examiner should also seek to mitigate burden by, wherever possible, using data in the form maintained by the institution.

General Guidelines

The primary objectives of conducting interviews with local community contacts are to:

- Gather information that might assist in the development of a community profile.

- Determine opportunities for participation by financial institutions in helping to meet local credit needs.

- Understand perceptions on the performance of financial institutions in helping to meet local credit needs.

- Provide a context on the community to assist in the evaluation of an institution's CRA performance.

This section provides information and procedures for conducting community contact interviews. It broadly addresses a wide variety of subjects to accommodate varying communities and types of institutions. As a result, it is **not** meant to be used in the order presented. Examiners should select those steps and procedures that apply to the unique circumstances of the institution or the community.

Coverage and Frequency of Community Contacts

Community contacts typically take the form of personal meetings. Telephone conversations or larger group meetings are permitted as necessary and appropriate. Information from other financial regulatory agencies will be provided in written form. (Although not implemented at the time of this writing, inter-agency community contact information may eventually be available in electronic form.) At least in conjunction with each examination, the OCC will make community contacts in the MSA, county, or assessment area(s) that the financial institution in question is serving. When possible, those community contacts should be made early in the examination to help to provide a context for evaluating the bank's performance.

Selection of Community Contacts

The number and nature of contacts will depend upon a variety of factors, including the complexity of the community, the size and type of the institution examined, and the amount and age of community-driven information already available to the examiner.

Treatment of Confidential Information

Confidentiality of Institution's Records

Examiners must maintain the confidentiality of any institution's proprietary information. When making community contacts, the examiner should not reveal any confidential information obtained from the institution's files or through discussions with management, or any conclusions drawn about the institution's performance or CRA rating.

Protection of Community Contacts

Maintaining the confidentiality of the community contact's identity, when requested to do so, is essential. Examiners must not reveal the name or other identifying information about a community contact to anyone outside the agency without the contact's permission to do so.

Report of Examination and CRA Performance Evaluation

Include in the report of examination and the CRA performance evaluation, as appropriate, a discussion of the number and kinds of CRA-related community contacts that were consulted and relevant information obtained and used, if any, in the CRA evaluation. Information should be factual. While opinions of contacts may be included when applicable, examiners should refrain from drawing conclusions or making judgements based solely on anecdotal evidence.

Sharing Information

The agencies routinely share information obtained during outreach contacts. Whenever community contacts are made, the examiner initiating the contact should complete the community contact form and submit it to the party designated within each agency. The designee will distribute copies of the form to their counterparts at the other regulatory agencies.

Preparing for the Interview

Before conducting interviews, review relevant background information to identify additional areas of inquiry. Adequate preparation for the interviews includes reviewing information on the assessment area, selecting community contacts and structuring the interview.

Reviewing Information on Assessment Area

Reviewing all available background materials before making community contacts is vital in developing a working understanding of the community you are about to enter. Establishing the nature, extent, and age of the information available before making community contacts helps to set the objectives of the community contact process. A well-developed context also allows for more detailed and in-depth community contact interviews. The examiner should:

- Assess prevailing economic conditions and demographic characteristics within and near the assessment area. This includes a review of available data on various population segments within the community; trends in migration, labor, and employment characteristics; comparisons to state and county/MSA data; and housing and real estate market statistics.

- Assess infrastructure and geographic characteristics within the assessment area. This includes a review of maps, natural areas, major thoroughfares, access to public transportation, locations of low- and moderate-income census tracts, names of specific low- and moderate-income neighborhoods, and proximity of the assessment area to military bases, airport facilities, and metropolitan centers. Internal mapping software, information from the financial institution, and information from local planning, transportation, economic development, or real estate boards are usually good sources of information.

- Assess distribution and availability of branch and ATM services especially with regard to low-income areas within the community. Include a review of check cashing facilities, if possible. (Internal mapping software, if available, can allow the examiner to map these locations.)

- Assess, to the extent information is available, local development issues and priorities in the areas of affordable housing, commercial activity, and economic and community development.

  A summary of such information may be available from the community affairs function. In addition, the examiner may wish to review previous community contacts for this locality including those from other regulatory agencies. If the examiner is reviewing a MSA, he or she should contact the city's municipality and obtain a copy of its consolidated plan (conplans). Conplans list the needs of an MSA as identified and prioritized by its officials. The examiner may also consider obtaining public reports from multiple listings services (MLS) and news articles on local development projects.

Quantitative sources may include feasibility studies, market analysis or commercial appraisal reports for local development projects. State or local economic development agencies, utility companies, real estate organizations, and universities present in the immediate or surrounding area are often good sources for such material. The section below, entitled "Identifying Potential Contacts" contains additional sources for these types of material.

- Determine the priorities of the community and the opportunities for financial institutions to participate with local governmental and nonprofit organizations in the areas of affordable housing, small business/farm development, and economic and community development. Review the number and nature of government agencies, nonprofit, and neighborhood organizations that provide programs and resources to the assessment area. If possible, note the amount of funds devoted to these purposes. Also, attempt to determine which programs or organizations are particularly active with respect to the low-income individuals or areas located in the assessment area.

  Sources of information for this step include previous community contacts in this area, information on local programs from the institution, and discussions with appropriate agency staff.

- Based upon information reviewed, above, identify areas that require further inquiry through the community contacts process. For example:

  — Are there any significant conflicting pieces of information that may require further investigation in the contact interviews?

  — Are there any pieces of quantitative information, such as housing and rental values, that are considerably outdated and need to be verified in the contact interviews?

  — Does the data suggest particular areas of "need" in affordable housing, such as housing rehabilitation, multifamily development, or single-family home purchase that you can investigate further and verify through the contact interviews? Alternatively, are needs for specific areas of the population, such as housing for the elderly, still unclear, requiring further study through the contact interviews?

- Does the data suggest particular areas of need in services such as ATMs, branches, or bilingual services that can be investigated further and verified through the contact interviews?

- Does the review identify organizations or projects requiring additional information?

Identifying Potential Community Contacts

This section discusses the number of types of community contacts that should be made during an examination. It also identifies potential community contacts and provides guidance on the sources of information that are available from them.

Number and Type of Contacts

Select contacts that can best provide information on the assessment area(s). Consider the nature of the information you are seeking to complete your analysis of the assessment area(s) and the purpose of the organizations in the assessment area(s). Examiners may wish to initially consult or select organizations on the telephone to determine which can best comment on particular issues.

Time constraints can limit the number of contacts that the examiner is able to make. The following factors may be considered when determining the appropriate number:

- The nature of any information provided by the institution including information that specifies credit, service, or community development needs in the institution's assessment area.

- The nature of public comments including information that specifies credit, service, or community development needs in the institution's assessment area.

- The amount of community contact information available from other examinations conducted in this area, both in number and substance, and the date the information was gathered.

- The complexity of the community including the size of its population, its geographic breadth, and the diversity of its population.

- The characteristics of the institution examined.

Organization Types

Grassroots Community Groups

Grassroots groups are formed when concerned individuals come together to solve common problems. Groups whose primary aim is to further the objectives of low-income residents are of particular interest. These groups can be difficult to identify because they tend to be smaller neighborhood groups and may not have readily recognizable names.

However, they will often share the following characteristics:

- Low-income representation is evident in policy and implementation aspects of organization. This may be evident at the board level, in the committee structure, or the day-to-day management.

- Input from low-income residents is clearly sought in functional/program aspects and information distribution to low-income individuals is a priority. Examples of this include door-to-door surveys and frequent neighborhood meetings.

- Low-income individuals are encouraged or empowered to solve problems collectively.

Types of organizations: Churches, block clubs, tenants association, low-income advocacy groups, housing or credit counseling programs, senior citizen groups, shelter providers, health clinics, and community network/collaborative groups.

Types of information available: Development priorities and concerns of the local low-income populations, available development programs and resources, current partnerships or development projects in the area, and the role of financial institutions in the assessment area.

Secondary information: Completed questionnaires or surveys.

Community-Based Development or Financial Intermediaries

The primary aim of these organizations is typically to increase the economic standard of low-income individuals or areas. Thus they tend to be involved in technical aspects of development such as residential and commercial real estate ventures or financing. Though these groups encourage representation of low-income individuals, they are also likely to have a higher degree of staff or decision makers that live outside of low-income areas that the organization is serving.

Types of organizations: Nonprofit organizations such as community development corporations (CDCs), church-based economic development programs, community loan funds, small business investment corporations (SBICs), specialized small business investment corporations (SSBICs); low-income housing organizations, technical assistance providers, low-income credit unions, development institutions, and microenterprise groups.

Types of information available: Low-income credit, service, and community development issues at the neighborhood level; quantitative information on housing values and actual real estate projects; qualitative information on financial institutions and financial practices of low-income individuals; technical details on financing and lending mechanisms for programs they offer; and information on other government and program resources or ventures in the community.

Secondary information: Feasibility studies, appraisal information on specific neighborhoods; local needs assessments; surveys of institutions' activity; surveys of financial practices of low-income clientele; and lending agreements by groups of local financial institutions.

Government Offices

Types of organizations include:

- Local branches of federal agencies such as the Department of Housing and Development (HUD), Small Business Administration (SBA), Department of Commerce Economic Development Administration (EDA), Farmers Home Administration (FmHA), the Bureau of Indian Affairs (BIA), and the Department of Agriculture (USDA).

- Local groups of federally funded or mandated programs such as: community action agencies (CAAs), neighborhood revitalization programs, Office of Minority Business Enterprise (OMBE) business development centers.

- Local elected officials such as mayors, commissioners, tribal chiefs, city council members, tribal council members.

- State and local housing agencies or authorities.

- Economic development agencies, including industrial and redevelopment agencies or authorities, county or regional planning agencies, transportation agencies, utility companies, rural electric cooperatives, economic development corporations (EDCs), local planning or economic development directors.

- School board superintendents and officials.

Types of information available: Types of loan, grant, guarantee, or other programs available for use by institutions and housing, community, and economic development groups, and the amount of funding available through such programs in the institution's assessment area(s); the extent to which local financial institutions participate in such programs and perspectives on barriers or issues related to their participation; specific project opportunities in which institutions could participate; information on underserved neighborhoods or areas.

Secondary information available: Housing, small business, agriculture, and general economic conditions and trends in the assessment area; publicly sponsored comprehensive or general development and redevelopment plans and maps; other plans and studies, such as housing plans (e.g., the consolidated plan), economic development plans and studies, and various community service needs in the assessment area. School boards can update census information by providing demographic information on the makeup of their student body. This information is typically collected annually.

Business and Labor Groups

Types of organizations: Chambers of commerce, downtown and neighborhood merchants associations, small and minority business advocacy groups, realtors, minority and nonminority real estate agents, local venture capital companies, SBA/college-supported small business development centers (SBDCs), feed stores, cattlemen's association, actual-small business owners, and small business technical assistance providers, such as business incubators, and local union representatives.

Types of information available: Data and perspectives on local business, economic conditions, recent economic activity and trends in the community; the nature and extent of small business activity, level of referrals from financial institutions to SBDCs; the existence of active SBA 504 program, SBIC, or SSBIC programs; perspectives on financial institution efforts to provide financing and services to small businesses/small farms; the level of institution participation in other public/private programs for small business development and employment training; other private and public sources of financing available for small businesses and small farms in the assessment area.

Secondary information available: Mortgage interest rate sheets from financial institutions or mortgage companies obtained from realtors.

Civil Rights and Consumer Protection Groups

Types of organizations include: Open housing/fair housing organizations, local chapters of the National Association for the Advancement of Colored People (NAACP), Urban League, Urban Coalition, and National Organization of

Women (NOW); legal aid/legal services offices; human relations commissions; state attorney general, consumer protection office.

Types of information available: Credit needs, issues, or priorities for any protected classes; complaints against specific financial institutions; general perspectives on financial institutions in the assessment area.

Secondary information available: Studies using testers in financial institutions, formal complaints or case write ups.

Other

Types of organizations include: Universities, research institutions, foundations, hospitals, or hospital extension programs.

Types of information available: Many and varied. Specific community projects by universities or hospitals may be involved.

Secondary information available: Demographic and economic data, independent research studies or reports on community development topics, studies and data collection on development and economic trends or opportunities in the area. Automated conplans may also be available.

Conducting the Interview

Having determined the groups or individuals to be contacted and the information to be solicited from each interview, the examiner must then plan the structure and content of questions before the interview. This section provides a sample list of questions that the examiner may wish to consider. The examiner should select and tailor questions from the list of sample questions that would be the most effective for each specific contact.

The questions highlight the type of information that the examiner is seeking through the community contact process. They are meant to serve as a guide to assist the examiner in planning the substance and structure of the interview. Obviously, not all questions will be appropriate to each specific contact. Nor is the list all inclusive; particular questions may generate significant discussions and examiners are expected to ask appropriate follow-up questions. Examiners are encouraged to review the entire list before structuring their interview. As examiners gain in experience, they are encouraged to engage in discussion with the community contact and not undertake a "question and answer" format.

Background Information on Community Contact

The examiner should ascertain the organization's area of expertise and the role that it plays in the community.

General

What geographic areas does the organization serve?

How old is the organization? How was it started? How much involvement by local residents, including low-income residents, was there initially?

Who does the organization represent? Roughly what percentage of your client base is very low-income (defined as 25 percent to 50 percent of median area income), low-income, moderate-income, or middle-income?

What is the mission and the primary goals of this organization? What are the goals for this year?

Is there a board of directors? What is the representation on the board? Are low-income neighborhood residents on the board? Are banks/lenders or other financial institutions on the board?

What projects or programs are you currently working on? Aside from programs are there other means in which the mission is carried out?

How many "clients" does this organization serve on a monthly or annual basis? If the organization is involved in development, how many real estate projects have been completed in the organization's history? How many are ongoing?

If direct loans have been provided through any programs, what type of loans are they? What segments of the community have benefited from these loans (very low-income, low-income, moderate-income, elderly, etc.)? What is the number and dollar volume of loans generated?

What are the amounts and sources of the organization's funding? How is the funding disbursed (i.e., what activities does it fund and how much of the budget is devoted to each activity)?

Could you list the organization's major accomplishments in the past five years? Is there such a list that you may have for purposes of your funders or funding proposals that I may have a copy of?

What are some of the limits the organization is facing in serving its community? In what areas is it currently encountering opportunity?

Is the organization interested in expanding its program or project areas at this time? In what area? Is there a time line in place to implement these activities, or is one expected to be in place?

Economic Development Contacts (Including Utility Companies)

Are there empowerment zones (EZs), enterprise communities (ECs), or foreign trade zones (FTZs) in your area? Where? What types of monetary incentives are offered?

What are examples of small business, small farm, and community-based development that the agency has been involved in? Has activity been concentrated in a few areas? Which ones?

Does the economic development agency also coordinate the housing program and monies for this jurisdiction? If not, is economic development coordinated with housing officials? What priority is accorded to affordable housing? What priorities, if any, are accorded to specific population segments (e.g., elderly, special assistance, female heads of households, homeless, other)?

Are the economic development strategies or the availability of the programs communicated to local residents in any way? How? [Note to examiners: did you find that local residents or community representatives were able to articulate strategies or various programs?]

Does the agency have working relationships established with community organizations at the neighborhood level? Who? What are the names of the individuals that the agency has worked with? If so, what is the extent of the partnership that has been established?

Local Government Contacts

What is the structure of the local government? Is there an economic development department? Is this separate from housing development?

Which department has responsibility for economic development policy?

Does the local government have programs that target affordable housing, small business development, or community development projects? How much funding do they have?

Has the local government identified priorities for its housing and economic development funds? Has the government determined what impact this will have for the population (e.g., for the elderly, low-income families, individuals with special needs, the homeless)? To the agency's knowledge, what has been the impact of its funds in the last several years?

How much money has been allocated for affordable housing, elderly needs, special needs, etc.? What is the time frame for the disbursement of funds, particularly CDBG funds?

Real Estate Broker Contacts

Do you have brokers who specialize in low- or moderate-income housing (single or multifamily)?

Obtaining a Community Profile

One of the primary objectives of the contact process is to update the community profile. The examiner is expected to obtain and update information on current economic conditions and trends, current demographic characteristics, and existing credit needs.

General

What is the current demographic makeup of the community? What were the most significant demographics changes in the past five to 10 years, if any (e.g., migration patterns, racial composition)?

Which neighborhoods are in transition, if any? Has gentrification or the displacement of low- or moderate-income individuals become an issue in certain neighborhoods? In which neighborhoods? Is the potential displacement of individuals being managed in some process, for example, a relocation package? If so, how and who is involved?

What major employers have either entered or left the community in the last few years? Has this affected certain categories of the labor market more than others? If so, which category benefited? Which category was hurt? How?

Who or what organizations are the driving forces in the community (examples include churches, government, community groups, etc.)?

What priorities have you identified for this area?

Have you conducted any studies (e.g., neighborhood surveys or feasibility studies) that may provide insight into local credit, service, or community development needs? What were the results? (Obtain a copy, if available.) How was the study used and what was the distribution (any banks included)?

Do zoning restrictions play a role in the availability of affordable housing units? How? Which neighborhoods are most affected?

Are absentee landlords a problem? For whom? In which neighborhoods?

In your opinion, what credit needs have not been adequately satisfied by area financial institutions? (Give examples such as small business loans, home improvement loans, installment loans, etc.)

To what extent are financial services available in the assessment area? What is the availability of ATMs or branches in this neighborhood?

Are there many women- or minority-owned businesses in the area? If so, are they concentrated in any geographic location or occupational field?

Community-based Organization Contacts

Does this community have a significant number of people that would be "uncounted" in official census figures? If so, why? Does your organization give estimates of the uncounted or real population?

What are the primary and secondary issues that low-income people in this area are concerned with in the short term? In the long term?

What are the most pressing concerns — e.g., adequate housing, access to retail goods, adequate public transportation facilities, adult education, job training and placement, English as a second language (ESL), health facilities — that you have been able to identify facing low-income residents?

What language(s) are spoken in the community?

Economic Development Agency Contacts (Including Utility Companies)

What are the primary economic strengths of this area? Primary weaknesses? (Note: Economic development agencies typically operate at the county or MSA level. Using follow up questions and probing techniques, attempt to get as local an assessment as possible.)

Are there development plans currently underway for infrastructure-related projects such as bridges, sewers, etc.? If so, what is the suggested time table? Will the project generate or is it generating jobs for low- or moderate-income residents?

What are the main economic development strategies (examples include business attraction, business retention, marketing, small business development, etc.) that you are currently pursuing for the overall county or MSA? For a particular neighborhood? What priority is given to small business, small farm, and community-based development (such as grocery stores, day care facilities, etc.)?

Housing Organization Contacts

What is the waiting list for various affordable housing programs in the area?

Have you received complaints from tenants that buildings are not in compliance with local building codes? In your perception, how widespread is this problem?

What is the demand for affordable housing? How does this compare with the availability of housing stock, both in terms of number of units and types of units?

How would you rate the need for housing among various sectors of the community, such as the elderly, individuals on special assistance, female heads of households, the homeless, others?

Are there structural inadequacies in the type of housing stock available for low-income populations in this area? Is housing rehabilitation a priority issue amongst those your organization has identified?

Real Estate Broker Contacts

What are the current economic conditions in this general area? Are housing values going up or down? If it is an "up" market, what are some of the forces contributing to its success? If down, what are some of the issues contributing to its decline? (Refer to specific geographic areas.)

Has there been any recent development activity in this area? What is the nature of the development (commercial, residential, affordable housing, public projects)? What has been the impact on the neighborhood?

Are there mobile homes or concentrations of mobile homes, such as mobile parks, in any area?

What is the average length of time that single-family homes are on the market in this neighborhood?

Are there other types of residences? Other neighborhoods?

Do you know of any changes in the near future that would impact the market for residential/commercial properties in a specific area? What are these changes (political, environmental, legal, etc.)?

Do you have copies of any appraisal reports for commercial and residential properties? For which areas? (Obtain when possible.)

Are you aware of appraisal-related problems in this neighborhood, such as the lack of comparables?

What credit products do your customers typically use to purchase a home? Conventional mortgages? Government loans? Land contracts? Why?

What are the various sources of financing that your customers typically use? Banks? Thrifts? Mortgage companies? Home improvement dealers? Credit unions? Employer-related sources (i.e., GMAC)? Others? Are particular combinations of sources more typical than others?

What are the characteristics of likely investors for multifamily housing properties in a specific neighborhood? What are the likely financial risks and rewards for investors in this area? (Compare with other neighborhoods.)

Foundation Contacts

What types of eligibility criteria are currently established for community development programs?

Which organizations and projects do you fund? How much money is committed to these organizations or projects for this year?

How long is the money committed for?

Out of the programs or organizations that you funded in this area, which are the most effective in the affordable housing area? In the small business development or community development area?

Assessing Opportunities for Financial Institution Participation

The degree to which financial institutions are involved in community development projects or services depends in some part on the extent of other resources and partners available within the community. Examiners are expected to obtain information on the availability of resources dedicated to the local credit or development needs that have been identified. Examiners are also expected to gauge the level of the contact's efforts in approaching local financial institutions and the mechanisms of any financing involved, if any.

In addition to any background materials reviewed in the preparation portion of the examination, contacts can provide relevant information on: the number and nature of community development or credit-related projects being developed for the benefit of the community, the number of organizations or government programs committed to those activities, the extent to which partnerships or other forms of coordination are evident in the area, the level of resources devoted to these activities, and how active these programs or resources are with respect to promoting the credit or banking needs that local representatives or residents have identified.

Community-based Organizations

Has your organization ever participated in activities, either formally or informally, with financial institutions? If so, which ones? For what projects or products? For what clients (e.g., what were the income characteristics of those who benefitted)?

Does your organization partner with other groups, including religious organizations, government agencies, and neighborhood organizations, in conducting any of its program activities?

Tell me about any other organizations you work with in meeting your clients' needs. What other organizations serve this community in the areas of affordable housing? Small business development? Commercial, day care, or other community-related facilities? Job training? Credit counseling? Low-income advocacy?

Which of these organizations do you consider most active? If I wanted more information from them, who should I contact?

Which financial intermediaries do you consider particularly effective? Why?

Are you seeking funds from local financial institutions for any current projects?

What is the nature of the project? Is it a development-based product? Is it related to credit needs in the community? Is there a specific neighborhood or group of individuals that this project will benefit? How?

What are the specific requirements for the financing that you are seeking?

Are you aware of similar projects that other organizations are working on? What can you tell me about those? Who can I contact to learn more?

Economic Development Agencies (State and Local)

What, if any, commercial development projects are underway? Where are they located? Are jobs created? Will low-or moderate-income individuals benefit? How?

What are the number and nature of the economic development programs funded by the city or state? How many residents do these programs benefit annually?

Which of these programs, if any, are designed to leverage funds from financial institutions? What are the mechanics of the program? How many projects have been funded to date? Which financial institutions have participated in these programs? Is there a particular area or group that these funds target?

Do you have programs designed specifically for affordable housing or small business development? If so, how many small businesses or small farms benefit? What is your definition of small business?

What are the funding levels of these programs? How many projects have been funded to date? Is there a particular neighborhood or group that these funds target? If so, what are they?

Have any financial institutions participated in these programs? If so, which ones?

Do you currently have other projects or have you had projects in the past that required either investment or other forms of financing from a financial institution? What are/were the characteristics of the project? What are/were the characteristics of its financing? (Include projects involving bond issuances, etc.) What were the results? Were the results innovative or risky?

What financing mechanisms are needed, are planned, or are in place for any development or infrastructure related projects?

Real Estate Brokers

Do you know about local or state financing programs for affordable housing, small business or commercial development? How did you hear of these programs?

Are there specific home insurance or financing programs that you utilize or to whom you refer customers? Which ones? Which do you utilize specifically for your low-income customers?

Which financial institutions in the area are you aware of that access these programs? How actively? Which do not?

Obtaining Local Perspectives on the Performance of Financial Institutions

Another function of the community contact process is to obtain feedback from the community on the performance of local financial institutions. The examiner is expected to gather information on the willingness and responsiveness of financial institutions, including the institution under examination, to work with local residents and professionals in meeting credit and community economic development needs.

General

With which banks, savings and loans, or mortgage companies have you been involved? What was the nature of your involvement?

Has your organization ever participated in activities, either formally or informally, with financial institutions? If so, which ones? How did this professional relationship develop?

What were the results of your involvement with financial institutions? In what ways has participation of the financial institution had a positive impact? In what ways has it had a negative impact? (Probe for such project aspects as timing, financing terms, etc.)

Are local financial institutions proactive in developing relationships or offering assistance? If so, which ones?

What financial institution(s) does your group recommend to your constituents? Why?

What obstacles, if any, prevent financial institutions from greater involvement in meeting local credit needs?

Have you ever been invited by institutions to participate in institution-sponsored activities? (If the answer is yes, specify the activities' purpose and the role you played.)

Has your organization ever received complaints about individual institutions?

Did the people affected know about the complaint process or were they informed about it?

Did any of the complaints involve allegations that the institution(s) discouraged people from submitting an application? Did any complaints involve geographic or racial redlining, or any other forms of discrimination? What happened?

Is anyone in your group or known to your group willing to offer specific evidence of discriminatory actions by specific institutions? (If allegations of discrimination, discouragement, or redlining are made with respect to an institution regulated by your agency, forward the relevant information to the institution's primary regulator.)

In your opinion, which institutions in the area have been particularly outstanding in meeting the community's needs? Why? What, specifically, has been done by these institutions?

In your opinion, which area institutions have been particularly notable for their unwillingness to respond to the community's needs? Why?

In your opinion, how well does (**institution name**) meet the credit needs of this community?

Community-based Organizations

Have you discussed local credit needs with any financial institutions? What were the results?

Do any institutions provide in-kind services, i.e, loaned executives, etc.?

What efforts are made to inform institutions and obtain their participation in the organization's activities? Which institutions participate and to what degree? Which institutions, if any, declined to participate?

If your organization works with government enhancement programs, do financial institutions work with you on that product? If so, which ones?

What efforts have you employed to improve your organization's relationship with any institutions? Which institutions? How successful have your efforts been?

Real Estate Brokers

Do you frequently work with financial institutions or other lenders that originate home mortgages? (Be sure to include those operating in low- or moderate-income areas).

Which institutions do you consistently receive rate sheets from? How are they typically delivered to you?

Are local lenders willing to work with you for first time home buyers? If so, which ones? Why or why not?

Are local lenders willing to work with you on exceptions on credit reports? If so, which ones? Why or why not?

What knowledge, if any, do you have of credit standards being adjusted in either a preferential or discriminatory manner? Which lenders? What were the circumstances?

Have you worked with lenders that have taken customers under the Fannie Mae 97 percent program? Freddie Mac? Others?

Which lenders do not receive your referrals for home purchases and why? Which lenders do not receive your referrals for small businesses and why?

What percentage of referred home buyers normally go to the recommended lenders?

What percentage of referred home buyers normally get loans from recommended lenders?

What other methods could be used to increase the use of insured financial institutions by people in your market area? In particular, are some financial institutions attracting portions of the market and not others? For which products?

Do women or minorities have more difficulty than men in obtaining mortgage loans? If so, why?

Which institutions are perceived as not meeting the needs of women or minority applicants?

Are there outreach activities by particular institutions for women or minority customers? Do you perceive these programs as positive?

In your experience, are there certain institutions favored in the minority or women's business community?

Business, Labor, or Consumer Groups Working with the Women or Minority Business Community

What is the general perception of financial institutions in the minority business community? Why?

In the women's business community? Why?

Do any financial institutions have a small business department targeting to woman or minorities? Which ones? How is it done?

Which institutions have separate minority or small business counseling services? Do the counselors also have lending authority?

Community Contact Form

Examiners should summarize each interview they conduct on the following community contact form. Its purpose is to provide a consistent means by which financial institution regulators can share information obtained through interviews for a particular community. The individual conducting the interview should inform the interviewee that this information will be shared with other regulatory agencies.

The interviewee has directed or authorized the interviewing agency's staff to:

☐ Never reveal his/her identity to persons outside the regulatory agencies.

☐ Not to reveal his/her identity at this time but to seek his/her permission when appropriate.

☐ Reveal his/her identity if the interviewing agency's staff determines that such a disclosure would be beneficial in enforcing relevant laws, regulations, or policies.

1. Regulatory agency _____
    District/regional office _____

2. Date of contact _____

3. Interviewee information
    Name_____
    Title_____
    Organization represented _____
    Type (see attached list)_____
    Address_____
    City_____ State _____

4. Was this the first contact with this organization made in connection with a current examination or as a follow-up contact?
    ☐   first   ☐   repeat

5. Was the interview conducted in conjunction with an examination? If yes, which one?

6. Summarize the organization's purposes, functions, and sources of funding. (Attach any literature, if available.) Include the organization's impact if applicable (for example, number of low-income clients served, number of units built, etc.).

7. Identify the boundaries of the political or geographic area served by the organization (may check more than one)

   ☐ state   ☐ county   ☐ MSA   ☐ city/town
   ☐ other_____

   In the area provided below, be specific about the names of any of the geographic entities identified above. If the institution serves smaller geographic areas, be specific about their location, including physical boundaries and names of neighborhoods wherever possible.

8. Summarize the interview into the following three categories using as many pages as needed. For more guidance on preparing the write-up, see the material under the Conducting the Interview section, above.

   Community profile: Current economic conditions; current demographic characteristics; general banking and credit needs; other (e.g., identifying names of low- or moderate-income neighborhoods).

   Opportunities for participation by local financial institutions: Community development, other credit-related projects, or financing programs; amount of opportunity for bank involvement.

   Performance of local financial institutions: Perceptions or experience regarding the degree of involvement of the local financial institution industry and of the specific financial institution (if obtained) in the community.

9. Person in charge of examination: _____

   Interviewer:_____

The format of the public evaluation follows the provisions of amendments to the Community Reinvestment Act that require the agencies to: (1) rate the institution's overall performance in meeting the credit needs of its community; (2) separately present the conclusions for each of the assessment factors the agencies considered in arriving at the rating as well as the facts and data supporting those conclusions for each metropolitan area in which the institution has branches; and (3) for interstate institutions, rate each state or multistate MSA in which the institution has branches.

The contents of the public evaluation will vary depending on the nature of the institution examined and the assessment method used. Samples of public evaluations for small institutions, large institutions, wholesale and limited-purpose institutions, and institutions operating under an approved strategic plan have been prepared by the agencies. These samples provide guidance regarding the structure and contents of the public evaluations. Except for the public evaluation for small institutions, the sample evaluations are structured to meet the requirements that the CRA imposes on public evaluations for interstate institutions. The samples can easily be adjusted to suit the requirements for institutions with branches in only one state, however.

Evaluations for Institutions with Branches in Only One State

Regardless of the assessment method used, the public evaluation for institutions with branches in only one state must contain the institution's overall CRA rating and the conclusions for the performance test(s) upon which the rating is based. If the institution has branches in more than one MSA, the public evaluation must present the conclusions for each of the performance tests, along with supporting facts and data, separately for each MSA. If the institution has branches in non-MSA areas of the state, the conclusions, facts, and data for those areas should also be presented.

More detailed discussions of each assessment area examined should follow the appropriate MSA and non-MSA presentation.

Evaluations for Interstate Institutions

In addition to the institution's overall CRA rating, the public evaluations for interstate institutions must contain ratings for each state and multistate

MSA in which the institution has branches. The public evaluation for interstate institutions is, therefore, organized to present the institution's overall rating first, followed by state and multistate MSA ratings. The discussion of the overall institution, state, and multistate MSA ratings must discuss the conclusions for the performance test(s) upon which the rating is based.

Separate MSA presentations for each MSA where the institution has branches should follow the appropriate state presentation. If the institution has branches in non-MSA areas within the state, a discussion of the statewide non-MSA area should also be included. Again, more detailed assessment area discussions follow the applicable MSA and non-MSA discussions.

Multistate MSA presentations should also be followed by discussions of the assessment area(s) within the multistate MSA to the extent that they are smaller than the multistate MSA. If the institution has delineated the multistate MSA as its assessment area, the detailed presentation of the assessment area and the institution's operations and performance should be contained in the discussion of the multistate MSA.

Conclusions Based on Performance Tests

The statute requires the agencies to present conclusions for each of the "assessment factors" considered in arriving at a rating. Performance tests have replaced assessment factors as the analytical tools for assessing CRA performance. The performance evaluations should reflect the conclusions reached under these performance tests.

For large, retail institutions, the public evaluation must indicate the conclusions reached under the lending, investment, and service tests. The streamlined assessment method for small institutions focuses on lending performance. To the extent that investment and service performance were considered in rating a small institution "outstanding," however, the conclusions for each must be placed in the public evaluation. Conclusions for the community development test must be discussed for wholesale and limited-purpose institutions. Finally, institutions that operate under an approved strategic plan may be assessed under one or more of the lending, investment, and service tests, depending on the plan. The performance evaluation for those institutions must contain conclusions for the tests used in the examination.

Hybrid Performance Evaluations

When an institution is examined under more than one assessment method, the examiner should develop a hybrid performance evaluation. The evaluation should state the assessment methods used in the "General Information" section. In addition, the discussion of the scope should indicate which method was used in each assessment area examined. Finally, discussions of the analysis used under each assessment area presentation should note the applicable assessment method.

Use of Charts, Tables, and Appendixes

Charts and tables should be used throughout the public evaluation to facilitate discussion of the institution's performance. In addition, the inclusion of one or more appendixes may facilitate the presentation of information in the public evaluation. For example, sample appendix A is a chart describing the scope of the examination and should be used for institutions with numerous assessment areas. Sample appendix B should be used to summarize the state ratings for interstate institutions. Other charts and tables may be used to assist the reader and amplify the discussion of an institution's performance.

Community Reinvestment Act
Examination Procedures

Large Retail Banks

Examination Scope

For all large retail banks (interstate and intrastate) with more than one assessment area (AA), select assessment areas for a full-scope review. In a full-scope review, examiners complete all of the procedures for an assessment area. For interstate banks, a minimum of one AA from each state, and a minimum of one AA from each multistate metropolitan area, must be reviewed using the examination procedures.

1. Review previous CRA performance evaluations, available community contact materials, and HMDA and CRA performance data including the bank's lending, investment, and service activities by assessment area, the lending of other lenders in those markets, and demographic information from those markets.

2. Select assessment areas for full-scope review by considering the factors below.

   a. The lending, investment, and service opportunities in the different assessment areas, particularly areas in which the need for bank credit, investments, and services is significant.

   b. The level of the bank's lending, investment, and service activity in the different assessment areas, particularly low- and moderate-income areas.

   c. The number of other institutions in the different assessment areas and how important the services of the bank under examination are to those areas, particularly any areas with few other providers of financial services.

   d. Comments and feedback received from community groups and the public regarding the bank's CRA performance.

   e. The size of the population.

   f. The existence of apparent anomalies in the reported CRA or HMDA data for any particular assessment area(s).

   g. The length of time since the assessment area(s) was reviewed.

h. The bank's previous CRA performance in its different assessment areas.

I. Issues raised during CRA examinations of other banks and previous community contacts in the bank's assessment areas or similar assessment areas.

Performance Context

1. Review standardized worksheets and other agency information sources to obtain relevant demographic, economic, and loan data, to the extent available, on each assessment area under review. Compare the data to similar data for the MSA, county, or state to determine how any similarities or differences will help in evaluating lending, investment, and service opportunities and community and economic conditions in the assessment area. Also consider whether the area has housing costs that are particularly high given area median income.

2. Obtain for review the consolidated reports of condition (call reports), annual reports, supervisory reports, and previous CRA evaluations of the institution under examination to help understand the institution's ability and capacity, including any limitations imposed by size, financial condition, or statutory, regulatory, economic or other constraints, to respond to safe and sound opportunities in the assessment area(s) for lending, investing, or providing services.

3. Consider any information the bank may provide on its local community and economy, its business strategy, its lending capacity, or that otherwise assists in the evaluation of the bank.

4. Review community contact forms prepared by the regulatory agencies and consult with district community reinvestment specialists to obtain information that assists in the evaluation of the bank. Contact local community, governmental, or economic development representatives to update or supplement this information.

5. Review the bank's public file and any comments received by the bank or the agency since the last CRA performance evaluation for information that assists in the evaluation of the bank.

6. By reviewing public evaluations and other financial data, determine whether any similarly situated banks (in terms of size, financial condition, product offerings, and business strategy) serve the same or similar assessment area(s) and would provide relevant and accurate information

for evaluating the bank's CRA performance. Consider, for example, whether the information could help identify:

    a. Lending opportunities available in the bank's assessment area(s) that are compatible with the bank's business strategy and consistent with safe and sound banking practices.

    b. Constraints affecting the opportunities to make safe and sound loans and qualified investments compatible with the bank's business strategy in the assessment area(s).

    c. Successful CRA-related product offerings or activities utilized by other lenders serving the same or similar assessment area(s).

7. Document the performance context information gathered for use in evaluating the bank's performance.

Assessment Area

1. Review the bank's stated assessment area(s) to ensure that it:

    a. Consists of one or more MSAs or contiguous political subdivisions (i.e., counties, cities, or towns).

    b. Includes the geographies where the bank has its main office, branches, and deposit-taking ATMs, as well as the surrounding geographies in which the bank originated or purchased a substantial portion of its loans.

    c. Consists only of whole census tracts and block numbering areas.

    d. Consists of separate delineations for areas that extend substantially across CMSA or state boundaries unless the assessment area is in a multistate MSA.

    e. Does not reflect illegal discrimination.

    f. Does not arbitrarily exclude any low- or moderate-income area(s) taking into account the bank's size and financial condition.

2. If the assessment area(s) does not coincide with the boundaries of an MSA or political subdivision(s), assess whether the adjustments to the boundaries were made because the assessment area would otherwise be too large for the bank to reasonably serve, have an unusual configuration, or include significant geographic barriers.

3. If the assessment area(s) fails to comply with the applicable criteria described above, develop, based on discussions with management, a revised assessment area(s) that complies with the criteria. Use this assessment area(s) to evaluate the bank's performance, but do not otherwise consider this fact in arriving at the bank's rating.

Lending, Investment, and Service Tests

Lending Test

1. Identify the bank's loans to be evaluated by reviewing:

   a. The most recent HMDA and CRA disclosure statements, the interim HMDA LAR, and any interim CRA loan data collected by the bank.

   b. A sample of consumer loans if consumer lending represents a substantial majority of the bank's business so that an accurate conclusion concerning the bank's lending record could not be reached without a review of consumer loans.

   c. Any other information the bank chooses to provide, such as small business loans secured by nonfarm residential real estate, home equity loans not reported for HMDA, unfunded commitments, any information on loans outstanding, and loan distribution analyses conducted by or for the bank, including any explanations for identified concerns or actions taken to address them.

2. Test a sample of loan files to verify the accuracy of data collected or reported by the bank. In addition, ensure that:

   a. Affiliate loans reported by the bank are not also attributed to the lending record of another affiliate subject to CRA. This can be accomplished by requesting the bank to identify how loans are attributed and how it ensures that all the loans within a given lending category (e.g., small business loans, home purchase loans, motor vehicle, credit card, home equity, other secured, and other unsecured loans) in a particular assessment area are reported for all of the bank's affiliates if the bank elects to count any affiliate loans.

   b. Loans reported as community development loans (including those originated or purchased by consortia or third parties) meet the definition of community development loans. Determine whether community development loans benefit the bank's assessment area(s) or a broader statewide or regional area that includes the bank's assessment area(s). Except for multi-family loans, ensure that community development loans have not also been reported by the bank or an affiliate as HMDA, small business or farm, or consumer loans. Review records provided to the bank by consortia or third parties or affiliates to ensure that the amount of the bank's third party or consortia or affiliate lending does not account for more than the bank's percentage share (based on the level of its participation or investment) of the total loans originated by the consortia, third parties, or affiliates.

   c.   All consumer loans in a particular loan category have been included when the bank collects and maintains the data for one or more loan categories and has elected to have the information evaluated.

3.   Identify the volume, both in dollars and number, of each type of loan being evaluated that the bank has made or purchased within its assessment area. Evaluate the bank's lending volume considering the bank's resources and business strategy and other information from the performance context, such as population, income, housing, and business data. Note whether the bank conducts certain lending activities in the bank and other activities in an affiliate in a way that could inappropriately influence an evaluation of borrower or geographic distribution.

4.   Review any analyses prepared by or for and offered by the bank for insight into the reasonableness of the bank's geographic distribution of lending. Test the accuracy of the data and determine if the analyses are reasonable. If areas of low or no penetration were identified, review explanations and determine whether action was taken to address disparities, if appropriate.

5.   Supplement with an independent analysis of geographic distribution as necessary. As applicable, determine the extent to which the bank is serving geographies in each income category and whether there are conspicuous gaps unexplained by the performance context. Conclusions should recognize that banks are not required to lend in every geography. The analysis should consider:

   a.   The number, dollar volume, and percentage of the bank's loans located within any of its assessment areas, as well as the number, dollar volume, and percentage of the bank's loans located outside any of its assessment areas (excluding affiliate lending).

   b.   The number, dollar volume, and percentage of each type of loan in the bank's portfolio in each geography, and in each category of geography (low-, moderate-, middle-, and upper-income).

c. The number of geographies penetrated in each income category, as determined in the step above, and the total number of geographies in each income category within the assessment area(s).

d. The number and dollar volume of its home purchase, home refinancing, and home improvement loans, respectively in each geography compared with the number of one-to-four family owner-occupied units in each geography.

e. The number and dollar volume of multi-family loans in each geography compared with the number of multi-family structures in each geography.

f. The number and dollar volume of small business and farm loans in each geography compared with the number of small businesses/farms in each geography.

g. Whether any gaps exist in lending activity for each income category, by identifying groups of contiguous geographies that have no loans or those with low penetration relative to the other geographies.

6. If there are groups of contiguous geographies within the bank's assessment area with abnormally low penetration, the examiner may determine if an analysis of the bank's performance compared with other lenders for home mortgage loans (using reported HMDA data) and for small businesses and small farm loans (using data provided by lenders subject to CRA) would provide an insight into the bank's lack of performance in those areas. This analysis is not required, but may provide insight if:

a. The reported loan category is substantially related to the bank's business strategies.

b. The area under analysis substantially overlaps the bank's assessment area(s).

c. The analysis includes a sufficient number and volume of transactions, and an adequate number of lenders with assessment area(s) substantially overlapping the bank's assessment area(s).

d. The assessment area data is free from anomalies that can cause distortions such as dominant lenders that are not subject to the CRA, a lender that dominates a part of an area used in calculating the overall lending, or there is an extraordinarily high level of performance, in the aggregate, by lenders in the bank's assessment area(s).

7. Using the analysis from step 6, decide whether the bank's abnormally low penetration in certain areas is a negative under the geographic distribution performance criteria of the lending test by considering:

   a. The bank's share of reported loans made in low- and moderate-income geographies versus its share of reported loans made in middle- and upper-income geographies within the assessment area(s).

   b. The number of lenders with assessment area(s) substantially overlapping the bank's assessment area(s).

   c. The reasons for penetration of these areas by other lenders, if any, and the lack of penetration by the bank being examined developed through discussions with management and the community contact process.

   d. The bank's ability to serve the subject area in light of (I) the demographic characteristics, economic condition, credit opportunities and demand; and (ii) the bank's business strategy and its capacity and constraints.

   e. The degree to which penetration by the bank in the subject area in a different reported loan category compensates for the relative lack of penetration in the subject area.

   f. The degree to which penetration by the bank in other low- and moderate-income geographies within the assessment area(s) in reported loan categories compensates for the relative lack of penetration in the subject area.

8. Review any analyses prepared by or for and offered by the bank for insight into the reasonableness of the bank's distribution of lending by borrower characteristics. Test the accuracy of the data and determine if the analyses are reasonable. If areas of low or no penetration were identified, review explanations and determine whether action was taken to address disparities, if appropriate.

9. Supplement with an independent analysis of the distribution of the bank's lending within the assessment area by borrower characteristics as necessary and applicable. Consider factors such as:

   a. The number, dollar volume, and percentage of the bank's total home mortgage loans and consumer loans, if included in the evaluation, to low-, moderate-, middle-, and upper-income borrowers.

   b. The percentage of the bank's total home mortgage loans and consumer loans, if included in the evaluation, to low-, moderate-, middle-, and upper-income borrowers compared with the percentage of the population within the assessment area who are low-, moderate-, middle-, and upper-income.

c. The number and dollar volume of small loans originated to businesses or farms by loan size of less than $100,000; at least $100,000 but less than $250,000; and at least $250,000 but less than or equal to $1 million.

d. The number and amount of the small loans to businesses or farms that had annual revenues of less than $1 million compared with the total reported number and amount of small loans to businesses or farms.

e. If the bank adequately serves borrowers within the assessment area(s), whether the distribution of the bank's lending outside of the assessment area based on borrower characteristics would enhance the assessment of the bank's overall performance.

10. Review data on the number and amount of the bank's community development loans. Using information obtained in the performance context procedures, especially with regard to community credit needs and institutional capacity, evaluate the extent, innovativeness, and complexity of community development lending to determine:

a. The extent to which community development lending opportunities have been available to the bank.

b. The responsiveness of the bank's community development lending.

c. How much leadership the bank has demonstrated in community development lending.

11. Evaluate whether the bank's performance under the lending test is enhanced by offering innovative loan products or products with more flexible terms to meet the credit needs of low- and moderate-income individuals or geographies. Consider:

a. The degree to which the loans serve low- and moderate-income creditworthy borrowers in new ways or loans serve groups of creditworthy borrowers not previously served by the bank.

b. The success of each product, including number and dollar volume of loans originated during the review period.

12. Discuss with management the preliminary findings in this section.

13. Summarize your conclusions regarding the bank's lending performance under the following criteria:

   a. Lending activity.

   b. Geographic distribution.

   c. Borrower characteristics.

   d. Community development lending.

   e. Use of innovative or flexible lending practices.

14. Prepare comments for the public evaluation and the examination report.

Investment Test

1. Identify qualified investments by reviewing the bank's investment portfolio, and at the bank's option, its affiliate's investment portfolio. As necessary, obtain a prospectus, or other information that describes the investment(s). This review should encompass qualified investments that were made since the previous examination (including those that have been sold or have matured) and may consider qualified investments made before the previous examination still outstanding. Also consider qualifying grants, donations, or in-kind contributions of property since the last examination that are for community development purposes.

2. Evaluate investment performance by determining:

   a. Whether the investments benefit the bank's assessment area(s) or a broader statewide or regional geographic area that includes the bank's assessment area(s).

   b. Whether the investments have been considered under the lending and service tests.

   c. Whether an affiliate's investments, if considered, have been claimed by another bank.

   d. The dollar volume of investments made to entities that are in or serve the assessment area, in relation to the bank's capacity and constraints, and assessment area characteristics and needs.

e. The use of any innovative or complex investments, in particular those that are not routinely provided by other investors.

f. The degree to which investments serve low- and moderate-income areas or individuals and are responsive to available opportunities for qualified investments.

3. Discuss with management the preliminary findings in this section.

4. Summarize conclusions about the bank's investment performance after considering:

a. The number and dollar amount of qualified investments.

b. Innovativeness and complexity of qualified investments.

c. The degree to which these types of investments not routinely provided by other private investors.

d. The responsiveness of qualified investments to available opportunities.

5. Write comments for the public evaluation and the examination report.

Service Test

Retail Banking Services

1. Determine from information available in the bank's public file:

a. The distribution of the bank's branches among low-, moderate-, middle-, and upper-income geographies in the bank's assessment area(s).

b. Banking services, including hours of operation and available loan and deposit products.

2. Obtain the bank's explanation for any material differences in the hours of operations of, or services available at, branches within low-, moderate-, middle-, and upper-income geographies in the bank's assessment area(s).

3. Evaluate the bank's record of opening and closing branch offices since the previous examination and information that could indicate whether changes have had a positive or negative effect, particularly on low- and moderate-income geographies or individuals.

4. Evaluate the accessibility and use of alternative systems for delivering retail banking services, (e.g., proprietary and nonproprietary ATMs, loan production offices (LPOs), banking by telephone or computer, and bank-at-work or by-mail programs) in low- and moderate-income geographies and to low- and moderate-income individuals.

5. Assess the quantity, quality, and accessibility of the bank's service-delivery systems provided in low-, moderate-, middle-, and upper-income geographies. Consider the degree to which services are tailored to the convenience and needs of each geography (e.g., extended business hours, including weekends, evenings, or by appointment, providing bi-lingual services in specific geographies, etc.).

Community Development Services

6. Identify the bank's community development services, including at the bank's option, services through affiliates, through discussions with management and a review of materials available from the public. Determine whether the services:

    a. Qualify under the definition of community development services.

    b. Benefit the assessment area(s) or a broader statewide or regional area encompassing the bank's assessment area(s).

    c. If provided by affiliates of the bank, are not claimed by other affiliated banks.

7. Evaluate in light of information gathered through the performance context procedures:

    a. The extent of community development services offered and used.

    b. Their innovativeness, including whether they serve low- or moderate-income customers in new ways or serve groups of customers not previously served.

    c. The degree to which they serve low- or moderate-income areas or individuals and their responsiveness to available opportunities for community development services.

8. Discuss with management the preliminary findings.

9. Summarize conclusions about the bank's system for delivering retail banking and community development services, considering:

a. The distribution of branches among low-, moderate-, middle-, and upper-income geographies.

b. The bank's record of opening and closing branches, particularly branches located in low- or moderate-income geographies or primarily serving low- or moderate-income individuals.

c. The availability and effectiveness of alternative systems for delivering retail banking services.

d. The extent to which the bank provides community development services.

e. The innovativeness and responsiveness of community development services.

f. The range and accessibility of services provided in low-, moderate-, middle-, and upper-income geographies.

10. Write comments for the public evaluation and the examination report.

Ratings

1. Group the analyses of the assessment areas examined by metropolitan area[1] and nonmetropolitan area for each state in which the bank has branches. If a bank has branches in two or more states of a multistate metropolitan area, group the assessment areas that are in that metropolitan area.

2. Summarize conclusions regarding the bank's performance in each metropolitan area and nonmetropolitan area of each state in which an assessment area was examined using these procedures. If two or more assessment areas in the metropolitan area or the nonmetropolitan area of a state were examined using these procedures, determine the relative significance of the bank's performance in each assessment area by considering:

a. The significance of the bank's lending, qualified investments, and lending-related services in each compared with the bank's overall activities.

---

[1] For purposes of CRA examinations and public evaluation, a metropolitan area is defined as MSAs, PMSAs, or CMSAs.

b. The lending, investment, and service opportunities in each.

c. The significance of the bank's lending, qualified investments, and lending-related services for each, particularly in light of the number of other banks in the area and the extent of their activities.

d. Demographic and economic conditions in each.

3. Evaluate the bank's performance in assessment areas not selected for examination using the procedures.

a. Revisit the demographic and lending, investment, and service data used to set the exam's scope. Consider the bank's operation (branches, lending portfolio mix, etc.) in the assessment area.

b. Through a review of the public file(s), consider any services that are customized to the assessment area.

c. Consider any other information provided by the bank (e.g., CRA self-assessment) regarding its performance in the area.

4. For metropolitan areas and the nonmetropolitan area of the state in which at least one assessment area was examined using the procedures, ensure that performance in the assessment areas not examined using the procedures is consistent with the conclusions based on the assessment areas examined in step 2 above. Select one of the following options for inclusion in the public evaluation:

a. The bank's [lending, investment, service] performance in the assessment area(s) is consistent with its [lending, investment, service] performance in the assessment areas within the state's [metropolitan area/nonmetropolitan area] that were reviewed using the examination procedures.

b. The bank's [lending/investment/service] performance in [the assessment area/these assessment areas] is [better than/worse than] its [lending/investment/service] performance in the assessment areas within [the metropolitan area/the nonmetropolitan area of the state] that were reviewed using the examination procedures; however, it does not change the conclusion for the [metropolitan area/nonmetropolitan area of the state].

5. For metropolitan areas and the nonmetropolitan area of the state where no assessment area was examined using the procedures, form a conclusion regarding the bank's lending, investment, and service

performance in the assessment area(s). When there are several assessment areas in the metropolitan area or the nonmetropolitan area of the state, form a conclusion regarding the bank's performance in the metropolitan area, or the nonmetropolitan area of the state. Determine the relative significance of the bank's performance in each assessment area within the metropolitan area, or the nonmetropolitan area of the state, by considering:

a. The significance of the bank's lending, qualified investments, and lending-related services in each compared with the bank's overall activities.

b. Demographic and economic conditions in each.

Also, select one of the following options for inclusion in the public evaluation:

a. The bank's [lending, investment, service] performance in [the assessment area(s)] is consistent with the bank's [lending, investment, service] performance [overall/in the state].

b. The bank's [lending/investment/service] performance in [the assessment area(s)] is [better than/worse than] the [lending/investment/service] performance for the [bank/state]; however, it does not change the [bank's/state] rating.

6. To determine the relative significance of each metropolitan area and nonmetropolitan area to the bank's overall performance (banks operating in one state) or statewide or multistate metropolitan area performance (banks operating in more that one state), consider:

a. The significance of the bank's lending, qualified investments, and lending-related services in each compared with the bank's overall activities.

b. The lending, investment, and service opportunities in each.

c. The significance of the bank's lending, qualified investments, and lending-related services for each, particularly in light of the number of other banks in the area and the extent of their activities in each.

d. Demographic and economic conditions in each.

7. Using the component test ratings chart below, assign component ratings that reflect the bank's lending, investment, and service performance. In

the case of a bank with branches in just one state, one set of component ratings will be assigned to the bank. If the bank has branches in two or more states and multistate metropolitan areas, component ratings will be assigned for each state or multistate metropolitan area reviewed.

Component Test Ratings	Lending	Investment	Service
Outstanding	12 points	6 points	6 points
High satisfactory	9 points	4 points	4 points
Satisfactory	6 points	3 points	3 points
Needs to improve	3 points	1 point	1 point
Substantial noncompliance	0 points	0 points	0 points

8. Assign a preliminary composite rating for the banks operating in only one state and a preliminary rating for each state or multistate metropolitan area reviewed for banks operating in more than one state. In assigning the rating, sum the numerical values of the component test ratings for the lending, investment, and service tests and refer to the chart below. No bank may receive an assigned rating of "satisfactory" or higher unless it receives a rating of at least "low satisfactory" on the lending test. In addition, a bank's assigned rating can be no more than three times the score on the lending test.

Composite Rating

Outstanding	20 points or more
Satisfactory	11 through 19 points
Needs to improve	5 through 10 points
Substantial noncompliance	0 through 4 points

9. Consider a bank's past performance if the previous rating was "needs to improve." If the poor performance has continued, a bank could be considered for a "substantial noncompliance" rating.

10. For banks with branches in more than one state or multistate metropolitan area, assign a preliminary overall rating. To determine the relative importance of each state and multistate metropolitan area to the bank's overall rating, consider:

  a. The significance of the bank's lending, qualified investments, and lending-related services in each compared with the bank's overall activities.

  b. The lending, investment, and service opportunities in each.

c. The significance of the bank's lending, qualified investments, and lending-related services for each, particularly in light of the number of other banks in the area and the extent of their activities.

d. Demographic and economic conditions in each.

11. Review the results of the fair lending component of the compliance examination and determine whether the findings should lower the bank's preliminary overall CRA rating or the preliminary CRA rating for a state or multistate metropolitan area. If evidence of discrimination was uncovered, consider the following:

a. The nature and extent of the evidence.

b. The bank's policies and procedures for preventing discriminatory or other illegal credit practices.

c. Any corrective action the bank took or committed to take, particularly voluntary corrective action resulting from a self-assessment conducted before the examination.

d. Other relevant information, such as the bank's past fair lending performance.

12. Assign final overall rating to the bank and discuss conclusions with management.

13. Write comments and conclusions, and create charts and tables reflecting area demographics, the bank's operation and its lending, investment, and service activity in each assessment area for inclusion in the public evaluation and examination report.

14. Prepare recommendations for supervisory strategy and matters that require attention for follow-up activities.

Public File Checklist

1. There is no need to review each branch or each complete public file during every examination. In determining the extent to which the bank's public files will be reviewed, consider the bank's record of compliance with the public file requirements in previous examinations, its branching structure and changes to it since its last examination, complaints about the bank's compliance with the public file requirements, and any other relevant information.

2. In any review of the public file undertaken, determine, as needed, whether branches display an accurate public notice in their lobbies and the file(s) in the main office and in each state contains:

   a. All written comments from the public relating to the bank's CRA performance and responses to them for the current and preceding two calendar years (except those that reflect adversely on the good name or reputation of any persons other than the bank).

   b. The bank's most recent "CRA Public Performance Evaluation."

   c. A map of each assessment area showing its boundaries, and on the map or in a separate list, the geographies contained within the assessment area.

   d. A list of the bank's branches, branches opened and closed during the current and each of the two previous calendar years, and their street addresses and geographies.

   e. A list of services (loan and deposit products and transaction fees generally offered, and hours of operation at the bank's branches), including a description of any material differences in the availability or cost of services between these locations.

   f. The bank's CRA disclosure statements for the two previous calendar years.

   g. A quarterly report of the bank's efforts to improve its record if it received a less than satisfactory rating during its most recent CRA examination.

   h. The HMDA disclosure statement for the two previous calendar years for the bank and for each nondepository affiliate the bank has elected to include in assessment of its CRA record, if applicable.

   I. If applicable, the number and amount of consumer loans made to the four income categories of borrowers and geographies (low, moderate, middle, and upper), and the number and amount located inside and outside of the assessment area(s).

3. In any branch review undertaken, determine whether the branch provides the most recent public evaluation and a list of services generally available at its branches and a description of any material differences in availability or cost of services at the branch (or a list of services available at the branch).

Lending Test Matrix

Characteristic	Outstanding	High Satisfactory	Satisfactory	Needs to Improve	Substantial Noncompliance
Lending activity	Lending levels reflect excellent responsiveness to assessment area credit needs.	Lending levels reflect good responsiveness to assessment area credit needs.	Lending levels reflect adequate responsiveness to assessment area credit needs.	Lending levels reflect poor responsiveness to assessment area credit needs.	Lending levels reflect very poor responsiveness to assessment area credit needs.
Assessment area(s) concentration	A substantial majority of loans are made in the institution's assessment area(s).	A high percentage of loans are made in the institutions' assessments area(s).	An adequate percentage of loans are made in the institution's assessment area(s).	A small percentage of loans are made in the institution's assessments area(s).	A very small percentage of loans are made in the institutions assessment area(s).
Geographic distribution of loans	The geographic distribution of loans reflects excellent penetration throughout the assessment area(s).	The geographic distribution of loans reflects good penetration throughout the assessment area(s).	The geographic distribution of loans reflects adequate penetration throughout the assessment area(s).	The geographic distribution of loans reflects poor penetration throughout the assessment area(s), particularly to low- or moderate-income geographies in the assessment area(s).	The geographic distribution of loans reflects very poor penetration throughout the assessment area(s), particularly to low- or moderate-income geographies in the assessment area(s).
Borrowers' profile	The distribution of borrowers reflects, given the product lines offered by the institution, excellent penetration among retail customers of different income levels and business customers of different size.	The distribution of borrowers reflects, given the product lines offered by the institution, good penetration among retail customers of different income levels and business customers of different size.	The distribution of borrowers reflects, given the product lines offered by the institution, adequate penetration among retail customers of different income levels and business customers of different size.	The distribution of borrowers reflects, given the product lines offered by the institution, poor penetration among retail customers of different income levels and business customers of different size.	The distribution of borrowers reflects, given the product lines offered by the institution, very poor penetration among retail customers of different income levels and business customers of different size.

Responsiveness to credit needs of highly economically disadvantaged geographies and low-income persons, small business	The institution exhibits an excellent record of serving the credit needs of the most economically disadvantaged area(s) of its assessment area(s), low-income individuals, and/or very small businesses, consistent with safe and sound banking practices.	The institution exhibits a good record of serving the credit needs of the most economically disadvantaged area(s) of its assessment area(s), low-income individuals, and/or very small businesses, consistent with safe and sound banking practices.	The institution exhibits an adequate record of serving the credit needs of the most economically disadvantaged area(s) of its assessment area(s), low-income individuals, and/or very small businesses, consistent with safe and sound banking practices.	The institution exhibits a poor record of serving the credit needs of the most economically disadvantaged area(s) of its assessment area(s), low-income individuals, and/or very small businesses, consistent with safe and sound banking practices.	The institution exhibits a very poor record of serving the credit needs of the most economically disadvantaged area of its assessment area(s), low-income individuals, and/or very small businesses, consistent with safe and sound banking practices.
Community development lending activities	The institution is a leader in making community development loans.	The institution has made a relatively high level of community development loans.	The institution has made an adequate level of community development loans.	The institution has made a low level of community development loans.	The institution has made few, if any, community development loans.
Product innovation	The institution makes extensive use of innovative and/or flexible lending practices in order to serve assessment area credit needs.	The institution uses innovative and/or flexible lending practices in order to serve assessment area credit needs.	The institution makes limited use of innovative and/or flexible lending practices in order to serve assessment area credit needs.	The institution makes little use of innovative and/or flexible lending practices in order to serve assessment area credit needs.	The institution makes no use of innovative and/or flexible lending practices in order to serve assessment area credit needs.

Investment Test Matrix

Characteristic	Outstanding	High Satisfactory	Satisfactory	Needs to Improve	Substantial Noncompliance
Investment and grant activity	The institution has an excellent level of qualified community development investment and grants, often in a leadership position, particularly those that are not routinely provided by private investors.	The institution has a significant level of qualified community development investments and grants, occasionally in a leadership position, particularly those that are not routinely provided by private investors.	The institution has an adequate level of qualified community development investments and grants, although rarely in a leadership position, particularly those that are not routinely provided by private investors.	The institution has a poor level of qualified community development investments and grants, but not in a leadership position, particularly those that are not routinely provided by private investors.	The institution has a few, if any, qualified community development investments or grants, particularly those that are not routinely provided by private investors.
Responsiveness to credit and community development needs	The institution exhibits excellent responsiveness to credit and community economic development needs.	The institution exhibits good responsiveness to credit and community economic development needs.	The institution exhibits adequate responsiveness to credit and community economic development needs.	The institution exhibits poor responsiveness to credit and community economic development needs.	The institution exhibits very poor responsiveness to credit and community economic development needs.
Community development initiatives	The institution makes extensive use of innovative and/or complex investments to support community development initiatives.	The institution makes significant use of innovative and/or complex investments to support community development initiatives.	The institution occasionally uses innovative and/or complex investments to support community development initiatives.	The institution rarely uses innovative and/or complex investments to support community development initiatives.	The institution does not use innovative and/or complex investments to support community development initiatives.

Service Test Matrix

Characteristic	Outstanding	High Satisfactory	Satisfactory	Needs to Improve	Substantial Noncompliance
Accessibility of delivery systems	Delivery systems are readily accessible to all portions of the institution's assessment area(s).	Delivery systems are accessible to essentially all portions of the institution's assessment area(s).	Delivery systems are reasonably accessible to essentially all portions of the institutions assessment area(s).	Delivery systems are accessible to limited portions of the institution's assessment area(s).	Delivery systems are inaccessible to significant portions of the assessment area(s), particularly low- and moderate-income geographies and/or low- and moderate-income individuals.
Changes in branch locations	To the extent changes have been made, the institution's record of opening and closing branches has improved the accessibility of its delivery systems, particularly in low- and moderate- income geographies and/or to low- and moderate-income individuals.	To the extent changes have been made, the institution's opening and closing of branches has not adversely affected the accessibility of its delivery systems, particularly in low- and moderate- income geographies and/or to low- and moderate-income individuals.	To the extent changes have been made, the institution's opening and closing of branches has generally not adversely affected the accessibility of its delivery systems, particularly in low-and moderate-income geographies and/or to low- and moderate-income individuals.	To the extent changes have been made, the institution's record of opening and closing branches has adversely affected the accessibility of its delivery systems, particularly in low- and moderate-income geographies and/or to low- and moderate-income individuals.	To the extent changes have been made, the institution's opening and closing of branches has significantly adversely affected the accessibility of its delivery systems, particularly in low- and moderate-income geographies and/or to low- and moderate-income individuals.
Reasonableness of business hours and services in meeting assessment area(s) needs	Services (including where appropriate, business hours) are tailored to the convenience and needs of the assessment area(s), particularly low- and moderate- income geographies and/or individuals.	Services (including, where appropriate, business hours) do not vary in a way that inconveniences certain portions of the assessment area(s), particularly low- and moderate-income geographies and/or individuals.	Services (including, where appropriate, business hours) do not vary in a way that inconveniences portions of the assessment area(s), particularly low- and moderate-income geographies and/or individuals.	Services (including, where appropriate, business hours) vary in a way that inconveniences certain portions of the assessment area(s), particularly low- and moderate-income geographies and/or individuals.	Services (including, where appropriate, business hours) vary in a way that significantly inconveniences many portions of the assessment area(s), particularly low and moderate-income geographies and/or individuals.
Community development services	The institution is a leader in providing community development services.	The institution provides a relatively high level of community development services.	The institution provides an adequate level of community development services.	The institution provides a limited level of community development services.	The institution provides few, if any, community development services.

Public Disclosure

(Date of Evaluation)**

Community Reinvestment Act
Performance Evaluation

Name of Depository Institution
Institution's Identification Number

Mailing Address of Institution

Name of Supervisory Agency

Address of Supervisory Office

NOTE: **This evaluation is not, nor should it be construed as, an assessment of the financial condition of this institution. The rating assigned to this institution does not represent an analysis, conclusion, or opinion of the federal financial supervisory agency concerning the safety and soundness of this financial institution.**

*   This is a sample created for a large, multistate institution and should be adjusted, as appropriate, to reflect the scope of the institution's operations. Refer to the "Instructions for Writing Public Evaluations" section of this booklet for further guidance.

**   Use the start date of the onsite examination reported in the type 02 or type 99 analysis that supports the CRA rating.

General Information

The Community Reinvestment Act (CRA) requires each federal financial supervisory agency, when examining financial institutions subject to its supervision, to use its authority to assess the institution's record of meeting the credit needs of its entire community, including low- and moderate-income neighborhoods, consistent with safe and sound operation of the institution. Upon the examination's conclusion, the agency must prepare a written evaluation of the institution's record of meeting the credit needs of its community.

This document is an evaluation of the CRA performance of **(name of depository institution)** prepared by **(name of agency)**, the institution's supervisory agency, as of **(date of evaluation.)** The agency evaluates performance in assessment area(s), as they are delineated by the institution, rather than individual branches. This assessment area evaluation may include the visits to some, but not necessarily all, of the institution's branches. The agency rates the CRA performance of an institution consistent with the provisions set forth in appendix A to 12 CFR part 25.

Institution's CRA Rating: This institution is rated _____.

Summarize the major factors supporting the institution's rating. When illegal discrimination or discouragement has been discovered and has affected the rating, the summary should state that the rating was influenced by violations of the substantive provisions of the antidiscrimination laws. The summary should not mention any technical violations of the antidiscrimination laws.

The following table indicates the performance level of (name of financial institution) with respect to the lending, investment, and service tests. (Indicate the performance level under each criteria by marking an "X" in the appropriate row.)

Performance Levels	Name of Financial Institution Performance Tests		
	Lending Test*	Investment Test	Service Test
Outstanding			
High Satisfactory			
Satisfactory			
Needs to Improve			
Substantial Noncompliance			

* Note: The lending test is weighted more heavily than the investment and service tests when arriving at an overall rating.

Description of Institution

Write a brief description of the institution. Include relevant information regarding the institution's holding company and affiliates, if any; the states and assessment areas served; the institution's ability to meet various credit needs based on its financial condition and size; product offerings; previous performance; legal impediments; and other factors. Other information that may be important includes total assets, asset/loan portfolio mix, primary business focus, branching network, and any merger or acquisition activity.

Conclusions about Performance Tests

Discuss the institution's overall CRA performance. The facts, data, and analyses that were used to form a conclusion about the rating should be reflected in the narrative, including the parts about institution strengths and areas for improvement. The narrative should clearly demonstrate how the results of each of the performance test analyses and relevant information from the performance context contributed to the institution's overall rating. Charts and tables should be used whenever possible to summarize and effectively present the most critical or informative data used by the examiner in analyzing the institution's performance and reaching conclusions.

Write a paragraph about the institution's record of complying with the antidiscrimination laws (ECOA, FHA, or HMDA) using the following guidelines:

- When substantive violations involving illegal discrimination or discouragement are found by the OCC or identified through self-assessment(s), state that substantive violations were found, whether they caused the CRA rating to be adjusted downward, and why the rating was or was not adjusted. Identify the law(s) and regulation(s) violated, the extent of the violation(s) (e.g., widespread or limited to a particular state, office, division, or subsidiary) and characterize management's responsiveness in acting to correct the violation(s). Determine whether the institution has policies, procedures, training programs, internal assessment efforts, or other practices to prevent discriminatory or other illegal credit practices.

- If no substantive violations were found, state that no violations of the substantive provisions of the antidiscrimination laws and regulations were discovered. Even if discrimination has not been found, comments related to the institution's fair lending policies, procedures, training programs, and internal assessment efforts may still be appropriate. If applicable, technical violations cited in the report of examination should be presented in general terms. Discuss whether management has [taken/proposed] steps that [have/would, if implemented,] address(ed) the technical violation(s).

Multistate Metropolitan Area

CRA Rating for (Name of Multistate MSA, including State names)[2]:_____
The lending test is rated: _____
The investment test is rated:_____
The service test is rated: _____

(Complete for each multistate metropolitan area where a bank has branches in two or more states within the multistate metropolitan area.)

Summarize the major factors supporting the institution's multistate metropolitan area rating. When illegal discrimination or discouragement has been discovered and has affected the rating, the conclusion should state that the rating was influenced by violations of the substantive provisions of the antidiscrimination laws. The conclusion should not mention any technical violations of the antidiscrimination laws.

Scope of Examination

Write a short description of the scope of the examination within the multistate metropolitan area. Discuss how CRA activities in the multistate metropolitan area were reviewed (using the examination procedures or through an analysis of available facts and data), and the time period covered in the review. When appropriate, you may also refer the reader to a chart similar to that included in appendix A.

Description of Institution's Operations in (Name of Multistate Metropolitan Area)

Describe the institution's operations within the multistate metropolitan area, including a description of each of the assessment area(s) that it serves within the multistate metropolitan area. Information that may be important includes total assets, asset/loan portfolio mix, primary business focus, branching network, and any merger or acquisition activity. For each of the assessment areas served, include key information such as the number of branches within the assessment area and the number of individuals and geographies in each income category. Indicate how many of those assessment areas were reviewed using the examination procedures. Other information that may be important includes population trends, type and condition of housing stock, available employment, and general business activity. Also summarize any

---

[2] This rating reflects performance within the multistate metropolitan area. The statewide evaluations are adjusted and do not reflect performance in the parts of those states contained within the multistate metropolitan area.

credit needs and lending opportunities that were noted. Discuss, if appropriate, the number and kinds of CRA-related community contacts that were consulted and any relevant information used in the CRA evaluation. Typically, more detailed information will be presented for assessment areas reviewed using the examination procedures. Charts and tables may be used to effectively present information as appropriate, particularly for assessment areas for which examiners do not use the examination procedures.

Conclusions about Performance Tests in (Name of Multistate Metropolitan Area)

Discuss the institution's CRA performance within the multistate metropolitan area, including institution strengths and areas for improvement. The narrative should clearly demonstrate how the results of each of the performance test analyses factored into the rating. Support your conclusions with an analysis of facts and data, such as the number and volume of loans and investments, by type, across geographies and borrower categories in the assessment areas reviewed using the examination procedures. When appropriate, support your conclusions with a discussion of the facts and data for assessment areas that were reviewed without using the examination procedures. State whether the institution's performance in the assessment areas reviewed without using the examination procedures is consistent with the institution's record in assessment areas reviewed using the examination procedures in the multistate metropolitan area. Charts and tables should be used whenever possible to summarize and effectively present the most critical or informative data used by the examiner in analyzing the institution's performance and reaching conclusions.

State

CRA Rating for (Name of State)[3]: _____

    The lending test is rated: _____
    The investment test is rated:_____
    The service test is rated: _____

(Complete for each state in which a multistate institution has branches if the institution has branches in two or more states. For an institution that has branches in only one state, complete the metropolitan area and nonmetropolitan statewide area presentations only for that state, as applicable in light of branch locations.)

Summarize the major factors supporting the institution's state rating. When illegal discrimination or discouragement has been discovered and has affected the rating, the conclusion should state that the rating was influenced by violations of the substantive provisions of the antidiscrimination laws. The conclusion should not mention any technical violations of the antidiscrimination laws.

Scope of Examination

Write a short description of the scope of the examination within the state. Discuss how CRA activities in the state were reviewed (which metropolitan areas or nonmetropolitan statewide areas included assessment areas that were reviewed using the examination procedures and which metropolitan areas were reviewed through an analysis of available facts and data) and the time period covered in the review. When appropriate, you may also refer the reader to a chart similar to that included in appendix A.

Description of Institution's Operations in (Name of State)

Describe the institution's operations within the state, including a description of the assessment area(s) served. Information that may be important includes total statewide assets; asset/loan portfolio mix; primary business focus; branching network; any merger or acquisition activity; and a brief description of the metropolitan areas, nonmetropolitan areas, and assessment areas served within the state.

---

[3]   For institutions with branches in two or more states in a multistate metropolitan area, this statewide evaluation is adjusted and does not reflect performance in the parts of those states contained within the multistate metropolitan area. Refer to the multistate metropolitan area rating and discussion for the rating and evaluation of the institution's performance in that area.

Conclusions about Performance Tests in (Name of State)

Discuss the institution's CRA performance within the state. The facts, data, and analyses that were used to form a conclusion about the rating should be reflected in the narrative, including the parts about institution strengths and areas for improvement. The narrative should clearly demonstrate how the results of each of the performance test analyses contributed to the rating. Charts and tables should be used whenever possible to summarize and effectively present the most critical or informative data used by the examiner in analyzing the institution's performance and reaching conclusions.

Metropolitan Areas
(For metropolitan areas in which some or all assessment areas
were reviewed using the examination procedures.)

Description of Institution's Operations in (Name of Metropolitan Area and State)

Describe the institution's operations within the metropolitan area, including a description of each of the assessment area(s) that it serves within the metropolitan area. Information that may be important includes the number of branches within the assessment areas and the number of individuals and geographies in each income category. Indicate how many assessment areas were reviewed using the examination procedures. Other information that may be important includes population trends, income levels, type and condition of housing stock, available employment, and general business activity. Also include a summary of any credit needs and lending opportunities that were noted. Discuss, if appropriate, the number and kinds of CRA-related community contacts that were consulted and any relevant information used in the CRA evaluation. Typically, more detailed information will be presented for assessment areas reviewed using the examination procedures. Charts and tables may be used to effectively present information as appropriate, particularly when the information is about assessment areas for which examiners do not use the examination procedures.

Conclusions about Performance Tests in (Name of Metropolitan Area and State)

Discuss the institution's CRA performance within the metropolitan area, including institution strengths and areas for improvement. The narrative should clearly demonstrate how the results of each of the performance test analyses contributed to the conclusion. Support your conclusions with an analysis of facts and data, such as the number and volume of loans and investments, by type, across geographies and borrower categories in the assessment areas reviewed using the examination procedures. When appropriate, support your conclusions with a discussion of the facts and data for assessment areas reviewed without using the examination procedures. Indicate whether the institution's performance in the assessment areas reviewed without using the examination procedures is consistent with the institution's record in assessment areas reviewed using the examination procedures. Charts and tables should be used whenever possible to summarize and effectively present the most critical or informative data used by the examiner in analyzing the institution's performance and reaching conclusions.

Metropolitan Areas

(For each metropolitan area in which no assessment areas were
reviewed using the examination procedures.)

Description of Institution's Operations in (Name of Metropolitan Area and State)

Describe the institution's operations within the metropolitan area and
characterize each assessment area that it serves within the metropolitan area.
Include such information as the number of branches within the assessment
areas and the number of persons and geographies in each income category.

Conclusions about Performance Tests in (Name of Metropolitan Area and State)

Summarize the facts and data that were reviewed, including demographic
information on the assessment areas and information on the institution's
performance. Indicate whether the institution's performance in the
assessment areas reviewed without using the examination procedures is
consistent with the institution's record [overall/in the state], using one of the
two following statements:

    a.   The institution's [lending, investment, service] performance in the
area is consistent with the institution's [lending, investment, service]
performance overall [or in the state].

    b.   The institution's [lending, investment, service] performance in the
area is [better than/worse than] the institution's [lending, investment,
service] performance for the [institution/state]; however, it does not
change the conclusion/rating for the [institution/state].

Nonmetropolitan Statewide Areas[4]

(When some or all assessment areas within the nonmetropolitan statewide area were reviewed using the examination procedures.)

Description of Institution's Operations in (Name of Nonmetropolitan Area and State):

Describe the institution's operations within the nonmetropolitan statewide area, including a description of each of the assessment areas that it serves within the nonmetropolitan statewide area. Information that may be important includes the number of branches within the assessment areas and the number of individuals and geographies in each income category. State how many of those assessment areas were reviewed using the examination procedures. Other information that may be important includes population trends, income levels, type and condition of housing stock, available employment, and general business activity. Also include a summary of any credit needs and lending opportunities that were noted. Discuss, if appropriate, the number and kinds of CRA-related community contacts that were consulted and any relevant information used in the CRA evaluation. Typically, more detailed information will be presented for assessment areas reviewed using the examination procedures. Charts and tables may be used to effectively present information as appropriate, particularly for assessment areas for which examiners do not use the examination procedures.

Conclusions about Performance Tests in (Name of Nonmetropolitan Area and State):

Discuss the institution's CRA performance within the nonmetropolitan statewide area. The facts, data, and analyses that were used to form a conclusion should be reflected in the narrative, including the parts about institution strengths and areas for improvement. The narrative should clearly demonstrate how the results of each of the performance test analyses contribute to the conclusions for the nonmetropolitan statewide area. Support your conclusions with an analysis of facts and data, such as the

---

[4] The discussion of an institution's CRA performance within a nonmetropolitan statewide area, is required only for institutions with branches in two or more states. A separate discussion of CRA performance within a nonmetropolitan statewide area for intrastate banks that have branches in metropolitan and nonmetropolitan areas is optional because the performance in the nonmetropolitan areas have been reviewed and discussed in the overall evaluation of the institution. Examiners may wish to discuss in greater detail, however, the assessment areas within nonmetropolitan areas that were reviewed using the examination procedures for intrastate banks with branches in metropolitan and nonmetropolitan areas, or for intrastate banks with branches only in nonmetropolitan areas.

number and volume of loans and investments, by type, across geographies and borrower categories in the assessment areas reviewed using the examination procedures. When appropriate, support your conclusions with a discussion of facts and data for assessment areas reviewed without using the examination procedures. Indicate whether the institution's performance in the assessment areas reviewed without using the examination procedures is consistent with its record in assessment areas reviewed using the examination procedures in the nonmetropolitan statewide area. Charts and tables should be used whenever possible to summarize and effectively present the most critical or informative data used by the examiner in analyzing the institution's performance and reaching conclusions.

Nonmetropolitan Statewide Areas[5]

(If none of the assessment areas within the nonmetropolitan statewide area
was reviewed using the examination procedures.)

Description of Institution's Operation in (Name of Nonmetropolitan Area and State):

Describe the institution's operations within the nonmetropolitan statewide
area and characterize each of the assessment areas that it serves. Include
such information as the number of branches within each assessment area and
the number of persons and geographies in each income category.

Conclusions about Performance Tests in (Name of Nonmetropolitan Statewide Area):

Summarize the facts and data that were reviewed, including information on
the assessment areas' demographics and the institution's performance. State
whether the institution's performance in the assessment areas reviewed
without using the examination procedures is consistent with the institution's
record [overall/in the state], using one of the two following statements:

a. The institution's [lending, investment, service] performance in the
   area is consistent with the institution's [lending, investment, service]
   performance [overall/in the state].

b. The institution's [lending, investment, service] performance in the
   area [is better than/is worse than], the institution's [lending,
   investment, service] performance for the [institution/state]; however,
   it does not change the conclusion/rating for the [institution/state].

---

[5] The discussion of an institution's CRA performance within a nonmetropolitan statewide area is
required only for institutions with branches in two or more states. A separate discussion of CRA
performance within a nonmetropolitan statewide area for intrastate banks that have branches in
metropolitan and nonmetropolitan areas is optional. Examiners may wish to discuss further the
assessment areas within the nonmetropolitan areas that were reviewed using the examination
procedures for intrastate banks with branches in metropolitan and nonmetropolitan areas or for
intrastate banks with branches only in nonmetropolitan areas.

Sample Appendix A: Scope of Examination

Write a short description of the scope of the examination. At a minimum, discuss the specific lending products reviewed, the names of any affiliates reviewed and their corresponding lending products, the institution's assessment areas and whether its activities in the assessment areas were reviewed using the examination procedures, and the time period covered in the review.

Large institutions with multiple assessment areas or affiliates subject to examination may warrant the use of charts that convey information regarding the scope of the examination. A chart such as the one on the next page may supplement or substitute for the discussion of scope.

Sample Scope of Examination

Time Period Reviewed			1/1/97 to 12/31/98
Financial institution XYZ State Bank, Grand Rapids, MI			**Products reviewed** Small business, small farm, consumer, unsecured
Affiliate(s)	**Affiliate relationship**		**Products reviewed**
XYZ Mortgage Company	Bank subsidiary		Mortgage loans
XYZ Community Investment Corp.	Holding co. subsidiary		Investments
XYZ Credit Card Corporation	Holding co. subsidiary		Credit cards
List of Assessment Areas and Type of Examination			
Assessment Area	**Type of Exam**	**Branches Visited**[6]	**Other Information**
Illinois MSA 0008 Decatur Adams County Non-MSA rural Illinois	 Full procedures Ltd procedures Full procedures		Mortgage loans not offered in non-MSA rural areas
Michigan MSA 0001 Grand Rapids City of Marcellus Non-MSA rural Michigan	 Full procedures Full procedures Ltd procedures		The scope of examination for non-MSA rural Michigan branches encompasses activities for the past six months, coinciding with the branches' acquisition date.

---

[6] There is a statutory requirement that the written evaluation of a multi-state institution's performance must list each branch examined in each state.

Sample Appendix B: Summary of State and Multistate MSA Ratings

State or multistate MSA name	Lending test rating	Investment test rating	Service test rating	Overall rating state/ multistate

Community Reinvestment Act Examination Procedures

Background and Purpose

Under the Community Reinvestment Act (CRA), institutions are evaluated on the basis of the product lines they offer in the normal course of business. Accordingly, wholesale institutions engaged in only incidental retail lending, and limited-purpose institutions offering a narrow product line to a regional or broader market, may request that they be assessed under the community development test. That test evaluates an institution's record of meeting the credit needs of its assessment area through community development lending, qualified investments, or community development services.

The Office of the Comptroller of the Currency's (OCC) CRA regulation provides that a national bank must first receive a designation as a wholesale or limited-purpose institution in order to be evaluated under the community development test. In order to receive such a designation, a bank must file a request in writing with the OCC (12 CFR 25.25).

A national bank will be evaluated under the community development test if its designation as a wholesale or limited-purpose institution is effective before the date of the commencement of the examination or evaluation. A national bank presently operating as a wholesale or limited-purpose institution should be prepared to be evaluated under the community development test as of the proposed effective date for the designation.

The provisions governing the process for requesting designation as a wholesale or limited-purpose institution are contained in the CRA regulation, 12 CFR 25.25. These guidelines do not supplant the regulation; rather, they are intended to serve as guidance in preparing a request for submission to the OCC. These guidelines specify the types of information that a national bank requesting designation as a wholesale or limited-purpose institution will generally need to submit. In addition to the items listed in the guidelines, a national bank may submit any other information that it may consider relevant to the OCC's decision.

The OCC will also review other relevant financial information, such as the Uniform Bank Performance Report (UBPR), Consolidated Reports of Condition (call reports), CRA and HMDA disclosure statements, supervisory reports, and previous CRA performance evaluations. This information is available in the OCC's supervisory data bases, however, and need not be submitted by the national bank.

Preparing and Submitting a Request

The designation request should be submitted, in writing, with the required information to the appropriate office designated by the OCC. For this purpose, the appropriate office shall be the Community and Consumer Policy Department. Inquiries concerning the preparation of a request for designation should also be directed to that office at the following address: Deputy Comptroller for Community and Consumer Policy, Office of the Comptroller of the Currency, Attn: CRA Designation, Washington, DC 20219.

The OCC may require the national bank to submit any additional statements or information it deems necessary. It is the national bank's responsibility to submit the information necessary to demonstrate that the request for designation as a wholesale or limited-purpose institution meets the criteria for approval.

Each designation request should name a contact person at the national bank. Upon receipt, the Community and Consumer Policy Department staff will review the request as submitted to determine if it is complete. A request will be deemed to be complete when all relevant information has been received by the OCC. If the request is deemed to be incomplete, the OCC will notify the requesting institution, and will send a request for additional information to the named contact person. If any information initially furnished with the request for designation changes significantly during the processing of that request, the national bank should communicate those changes promptly to the Community and Consumer Policy Department.

Each request for designation should also contain a proposed effective date. The proposed effective date should be at least 90 days after the request for designation is submitted to the OCC.

OCC Notification of Decision

The OCC will notify the bank in writing of its decision to approve or deny the request within 60 days of receiving a complete written request. If approved, the designation remains in effect until the national bank requests revocation of the designation or until one year after the OCC notifies the bank that the OCC has revoked the designation on its own initiative.

Confidentiality

Under the provisions of the Freedom of Information Act (FOIA), 5 USC 552, a request for designation as a wholesale or limited-purpose institution that is submitted to the OCC is a public document and is available to the public upon request. The OCC's decision approving or denying a request for designation may also be available to the public under the FOIA.

A national bank may request confidential treatment for information that would be exempt from the FOIA disclosure requirements. For example, if the requesting institution is of the opinion that disclosure of commercial or financial information would likely result in substantial harm to its competitive position or that of its affiliates, or that disclosure of information of a personal nature would result in a clearly unwarranted invasion of personal privacy, confidential treatment of such information may be requested. This request for confidential treatment must be submitted in writing concurrently with the filing of the request for designation as a wholesale or limited-purpose institution and must discuss in detail the justification for confidential treatment. Justification must be provided for each category of information for which confidential treatment is requested. The institution's request for confidentiality should explain the harm that would result from public release of the information.

Information for which confidential treatment is sought should be: (1) segregated from the other information that is submitted; (2) specifically identified in the nonconfidential portion of the designation request (by reference to the confidential section); and (3) labeled "Confidential." The requesting national bank should follow this same procedure on confidentiality with regard to filing any supplemental information. The OCC will determine whether information labeled confidential will be so regarded, and will advise the requesting national bank of any decision to make information labeled confidential available to the public.

A national bank should follow the rules stated above when submitting confidential supervisory information, which includes any information contained in, related to, or derived from reports of examination and inspection, or confidential operating and condition reports.

Requested Information

1. A request for designation as a wholesale or limited-purpose institution should state how the national bank satisfies one of the following definitions:

    Wholesale institution: An institution that is not in the business of extending home mortgage, small-business, small-farm, or consumer loans to retail customers. An institution will not be considered in the business of extending loans to retail customers if it does not hold itself out to the retail public as providing such loans and the institution's revenues from extending such loans are insignificant when compared with its overall lending operations. Wholesale institutions may engage in very limited retail lending, if this activity is incidental and is done on an accommodation basis.

> **Limited-purpose institution**: An institution that offers only a narrow product line (such as credit cards or automobile loans) to a regional or broader market. A limited-purpose institution continues to meet the narrow product line requirement if it only infrequently provides other types of loans.

A so-called "niche institution," (an institution that is in the business of lending to the public, but that specializes in certain types of retail loans or extending credit to a group of borrowers with, for example, certain financial or professional characteristics) generally would not qualify as a wholesale or limited-purpose institution. A savings association or savings bank generally would not qualify as a limited-purpose institution absent additional limitations on its activities.

The statement should contain facts and data sufficient to describe the nature of the national bank's current and prospective business, credit products offered, and the market area served. For a de novo national bank, the written request must include a business plan that contains a description of the institution's proposed nature of business, credit and other product(s) to be offered, and the market area to be served.

2. If the national bank engages in retail or other lending activities that may not be viewed as consistent with its request for designation as a wholesale or limited-purpose institution, it should provide sufficient information about those activities to allow the OCC to determine whether they are infrequent, incidental, or performed on an accommodation basis. This information should address the following elements, as appropriate:

   a. Describe each type of activity and the conditions or circumstances under which the national bank offers the product or service. For example, if the national bank engages in mortgage lending, explain whether such loans are offered to the general public or, for example, are offered only to corporate customers or employees of the institution.

   b. State the percentage of the national bank's assets and income that each activity represents.

   c. Explain how the incidental lending activity relates to the national bank's assessment area(s).

d. State whether the volume of incidental lending activity would be sufficient to allow for a reasonable evaluation of the national bank's performance under the lending test.

3. Describe any legal constraints or limitations that affect the type of credit services that the national bank may offer.

4. Describe the national bank's assessment area(s) and the location of its branches and offices. The national bank's assessment area(s) generally must consist of one or more MSAs or one or more contiguous political subdivisions in which the institution has its main office, branches, and deposit taking ATMs.

5. Explain how the national bank's network of branches is consistent with the designation as a wholesale or limited-purpose institution.

6. State the proposed effective date for the designation, which should be at least 90 days after the request is submitted to the OCC.

Examination Scope

1. For institutions with more than one assessment area, select assessment areas for an on-site examination. To select one or more assessment areas for an on-site examination, review previous performance evaluations, available community contact materials, reported lending data and demographic data on each assessment area and consider factors such as:

   a. The lending, investment, and service activity in the different assessment areas, particularly community development activities.

   b. The lending, investment, and service opportunities available in the different assessment areas, particularly community development opportunities.

   c. The length of time since the most recent on-site review of the assessment area(s).

   d. The institution's previous CRA performance in different assessment areas.

   e. The number of other institutions in the assessment areas and the importance of the institution under examination in addressing community development needs in the different assessment areas, particularly in areas with a limited number of financial service providers.

   f. The existence of apparent anomalies in the reported HMDA data for any particular assessment area.

   g. The findings of examiners in the same or similar assessment areas.

   h. Comments from the public regarding the institution's CRA performance.

2. For interstate institutions, a rating must be assigned for each state in which the institution has a branch and for each multistate MSA where the institution has branches in two or more of the states that comprise the multistate MSA. Select one or more assessment areas in each state for examination using these procedures.

Performance Context

1. Review standardized worksheets and other agency information sources to obtain relevant demographic, economic, and loan data, to the extent available, on each assessment area under review. Consider, among other things, whether housing costs are particularly high in relation to area median income.

2. Consider any information the institution may provide on its local community and economy and its community development lending, investment, and service capacity or that otherwise assists in the evaluation of the institution's community development activities.

3. Review community contact forms prepared by the regulatory agencies and consult with district community reinvestment and development specialists to obtain information that assists in the evaluation of the institution's community development activities. Contact local community, government, or economic development representatives to update or supplement information about community development activities in the assessment area(s) or the broader statewide or regional areas of which the assessment area(s) is a part.

4. Identify barriers, if any, to participation by the institution in local community development activities. For example, evaluate the institution's ability and capacity to help meet the community development needs of its assessment area(s) through a review of the Uniform Bank Performance Report (UBPR), the Consolidated Report of Condition (call report), annual reports, supervisory reports, previous CRA performance evaluations, and financial information for other wholesale/limited-purpose institutions serving approximately the same assessment area(s).

5. Review the institution's public file and any comments received by the institution or the agency since the last CRA performance evaluation for information that assists in the evaluation of the institution.

6. Document the performance context information gathered for use in evaluating the institution's CRA record.

Assessment Area

1. Review the institution's stated assessment area(s) to ensure that it:

   a. Consists of one or more MSAs or contiguous political subdivisions (i.e., counties, cities, or towns) where the institution has its main office, branches, and deposit-taking ATMs.

   b. Consists only of whole census tracts and block numbering areas.

   c. Consists of separate delineations for areas that extend substantially across CMSA or state boundaries unless the assessment area is located in a multistate MSA.

   d. Does not reflect illegal discrimination.

   e. Does not arbitrarily exclude any low- or moderate-income area(s) taking into account the institution's size and financial condition.

2. If the assessment area(s) does not coincide with the boundaries of an MSA or political subdivision(s), assess whether the adjustments to the boundaries were made because the assessment area would otherwise be too large for the institution to reasonably serve, have an unusual configuration, or include significant geographic barriers.

3. If the assessment area(s) fails to comply with the applicable criteria described above, develop, based on discussions with management, a revised assessment area(s) that complies with the criteria. Use this assessment area(s) to evaluate the institution's performance, but do not otherwise consider the revision in determining the institution's rating.

Community Development Test

1. Identify the number and amount of the institution's community development loans (originations and purchases of loans and any other data the institution chooses to provide), qualified investments, and community development services. Obtain this information through discussions with management, a review of the CRA disclosure statements and the HMDA-LAR, as applicable; any interim CRA disclosure data or HMDA data, collected by the institution, as applicable; investment portfolios; any other relevant financial records; and materials available to the public. Include, at the institution's option:

a. Qualified investments, community development loans and community development services provided by affiliates, if they are not claimed by any other institution.

b. Community development lending by consortia or third parties.

2. Test a sample of community development loan files to verify that they qualify as community development loans.

3. If the institution participates in community development lending by consortia or third parties, or claims activities provided by affiliates, review records provided to the institution by the consortia or third parties or affiliates to ensure that the community development loans claimed by the institution do not account for more than the institution's share (based on the level of its participation or investment) of the total loans originated by the consortium or third party.

4. Considering the institution's capacity and constraints and other information obtained through the performance context review, form conclusions about:

a. The extent, by number and volume, of community development loans, services, and qualified investments.

b. The degree of innovation in community development activities (e.g., serving low- or moderate-income borrowers in new ways or serving groups of creditworthy borrowers not previously served by the institution).

c. The complexity of those community development activities, such as the use of enhancements or other features specifically designed to expand community development lending.

d. The responsiveness to the opportunities for community development lending, qualified investments, and community development services.

e. The degree to which the institution's qualified investments serve needs not routinely provided by other private investors.

5. Summarize conclusions regarding the institution's community development performance and retain in the work papers.

Ratings

1. Review the analyses of the institution's performance in each assessment area examined, considering only those community development activities

---

that benefit the assessment area(s) and the broader statewide or regional area(s) that include the assessment area(s).

2. Group the analyses of the assessment areas examined by MSA and non-MSA areas within each state where the institution has branches. If an institution has branches in two or more states of a multistate MSA, group the assessment areas in that MSA.

3. Summarize conclusions about the institution's performance in each MSA and the non-MSA portion of each state in which an assessment area was examined using these procedures. If two or more assessment areas in an MSA or in the non-MSA portion of a state were examined using these procedures, determine the relative significance of the institution's performance in each assessment area by considering:

    a. The significance of the institution's activities in each compared with the institution's overall activities.

    b. The community development opportunities in each.

    c. The significance of the institution's activities for each, particularly in light of the number of other institutions and the extent of their activities in each.

    d. Demographic and economic conditions in each.

4. For assessment areas in MSAs and non-MSA areas that were not examined, consider facts and data related to the institution's community development lending, investment, and service activities to ensure that performance in those areas is consistent with the conclusions based on the assessment areas examined.

5. Assign a preliminary rating for an institution with operations in one state only using the "Community Development Ratings Matrix." For an institution with operations in more than one state or multistate MSA, assign a preliminary rating for each state using the Community Development Ratings Matrix. To determine the relative significance of each MSA and non-MSA area to the institution's overall rating (institutions operating in only one state) or state-wide or multistate MSA rating (institutions operating in more that one state), consider:

    a. The significance of the institution's activities in each compared with the institution's overall activities.

b. The community development opportunities in each.

c. The significance of the institution's activities for each, particularly in light of the number of other institutions and the extent of their activities in each.

d. Demographic and economic conditions in each.

6. For institutions with operations in more than one state or multistate MSA, assign a preliminary rating for the institutions as a whole. To determine the relative significance of each state or multistate MSA consider:

a. The significance of the institution's activities in each compared with the institution's overall activities.

b. The community development opportunities in each.

c. The significance of the institution's activities for each, particularly in light of the number of other institutions and the extent of their activities in each.

d. Demographic and economic conditions in each.

7. If the institution is adequately meeting the community development needs of each of its assessment area(s), consider those community development activities, if any, that benefit areas outside of the assessment area(s) or a broader statewide or regional area that includes the assessment area(s). Determine whether those activities enhance the preliminary rating. If so, adjust the rating(s) accordingly.

8. Consider an institution's past performance if the previous rating was "needs to improve." If the poor performance has continued, an institution could be considered for a "substantial noncompliance" rating.

9. Review the results of the fair lending component of the compliance examination and determine whether the findings should lower, in the case of an institution with operations in just one state, the institution's preliminary composite rating. In the case of an institution with operations in more than one state or in multistate MSAs, determine whether the findings should lower any of the preliminary state ratings or the preliminary composite rating. In considering the impact of evidence of discrimination on a state or composite rating, consider the following:

a. The nature and extent of the evidence.

b. The policies and procedures that the institution has in place to prevent discriminatory or other illegal credit practices.

c. Any corrective action the institution took or committed to take, particularly voluntary corrective action resulting from a self-assessment conducted before the examination.

d. Other relevant information, such as the institution's past fair lending performance.

10. Assign a final composite rating to the institution and discuss conclusions with management.

11. Write comments for the public evaluation and examination report.

12. Prepare recommendations for supervisory strategy and matters that require attention for follow-up activities.

Public File Checklist

1. There is no need to review each branch or each complete public file in every examination. When determining the extent to which the public files should be reviewed, consider the institution's record of compliance with the public file requirements in previous examinations, its branching structure and changes to it since its last examination, complaints about the institution's compliance with the public file requirements, and any other relevant information.

2. In any review of the public file undertaken, determine, as needed, whether branches display an accurate public notice in their lobbies, a complete public file is available in the institution's main office and at least one branch in each state, and the public file(s) in the main office and in each state contain:

a. All written comments from the public relating to the institution's CRA performance and any responses to them for the current and preceding two calendar years (except those that reflect adversely on the good name or reputation of any persons other than the institution).

b. The institution's most recent CRA performance evaluation.

c. A map of each assessment area showing its boundaries and, on the map or in a separate list, the geographies contained within the assessment area.

d. A list of the institution's branches, branches opened and closed during the current and each of the two previous calendar years, their street addresses and geographies.

e. A list of services (loan and deposit products and transaction fees) generally offered, and hours of operation at the institution's branches, including a description of any material differences in the availability or cost of services between those locations.

f. The institution's CRA disclosure statement(s) for the two previous calendar years.

g. A quarterly updated progress report describing the institution's efforts to improve its performance if it received a less than satisfactory rating during its most recent CRA examination.

h. HMDA disclosure statements for the two previous calendar years and those of each nondepository affiliate the institution has elected to include in the assessment of its CRA record, if applicable.

I. If applicable, the number and amount of consumer loans made to the four income categories of borrowers and geographies (low, moderate, middle, and upper) located inside and outside of the assessment area(s).

3. In any branch review undertaken, determine whether the branch provides the most recent public evaluation and a list of services generally available at its branches and a description of any material differences in the availability or cost of services at the branch (or a list of services available at the branch).

COMMUNITY DEVELOPMENT TEST MATRIX

CHARACTERISTIC	OUTSTANDING	SATISFACTORY	NEEDS TO IMPROVE	SUBSTANTIAL NON-COMPLIANCE
Investment, Loan, and Service Activity	The institution has a high level of community development loans, community development services, or qualified investments, particularly investments that are not routinely provided by private investors.	The institution has an adequate level of community development loans, community development services, or qualified investments, particularly investments that are not routinely provided by private investors.	The institution has a poor level of community development loans, community development services, or qualified investments, particularly investments that are not routinely provided by private investors.	The institution has few, if any, community development loans, community development services, or qualified investments, particularly investments that are not routinely provided by private investors.
Investment, Loan, and Service Initiatives	The institution extensively uses innovative or complex qualified investments, community development loans, or community development services.	The institution occasionally uses innovative or complex qualified investments, community development loans, or community development services.	The institution rarely uses innovative or complex qualified investments, community development loans, or community development services.	The institution does not use innovative or complex qualified investments, community development loans, or community development services.
Responsiveness to community development needs	The institution exhibits excellent responsiveness to credit and community economic development needs in its assessment area(s).	The institution exhibits adequate responsiveness to credit and community economic development needs in its assessment area(s).	The institution exhibits poor responsiveness to credit and community economic needs in its assessment area(s).	The institution exhibits very poor responsiveness to credit and community economic development needs in its assessment area(s).

Public Disclosure

(Date of Evaluation)**

Community Reinvestment Act
Performance Evaluation

Name of Depository Institution
Institution's Identification Number

Mailing Address of Institution

Name of Supervisory Agency

Address of Supervisory Office

Note: **This evaluation is not, nor should it be construed as, an assessment of the financial condition of this institution. The rating assigned to this institution does not represent an analysis, conclusion, or opinion of the federal financial supervisory agency concerning the safety and soundness of this financial institution.**

* This is a sample created for a large, multistate institution and should be adjusted, as appropriate, to reflect the scope of the institution's operations. Refer to the "Instructions for Writing Public Evaluations" section of this booklet for further guidance.

** Use the start date of the onsite examination reported in the type 02 or type 99 analysis that supports the CRA rating.

General Information

The Community Reinvestment Act (CRA) requires each federal financial supervisory agency to use its authority when examining financial institutions subject to its supervision, to assess the institution's record of meeting the credit needs of its entire community, including low- and moderate-income neighborhoods, consistent with safe and sound operation of the institution. Upon conclusion of such examination, the agency must prepare a written evaluation of the institution's record of meeting the credit needs of its community.

This document is an evaluation of the CRA performance of **(name of depository institution)** prepared by **(name of agency)**, the institution's supervisory agency, as of **(date of examination)**. The agency evaluates performance in assessment area(s), as they are delineated by the institution, rather than individual branches. This assessment area evaluation may include the visits to some, but not necessarily all of the institution's branches. The agency rates the CRA performance of an institution consistent with the provisions set forth in appendix A to 12 CFR part 25.

Institution's CRA Rating: This institution is rated _____.

Summarize the major factors supporting the institution's rating. When illegal discrimination or discouragement has been identified and has affected the rating, the summary should include a statement that the rating was influenced by violations of the substantive provisions of the antidiscrimination laws. The summary should not mention any technical violations of the antidiscrimination laws.

Description of Institution

Write a brief description of the institution. Include relevant information regarding the institution's holding company and affiliates, if any, the states and assessment areas served, the institution's ability to meet various credit needs based on its financial condition and size, product offerings, previous performance, legal impediments and other factors. Other information that may be important includes total assets, asset/loan portfolio mix, primary business focus, branching network, and any merger or acquisition activity.

Conclusions about Performance

Discuss the institution's overall CRA performance. The facts, data, and analyses that were used to determine the overall rating should be reflected in the narrative, including institution strengths and areas for improvement. The narrative should clearly demonstrate how the analyses of each of the performance criteria, and relevant information from the performance context, was factored into the overall institution rating. Discuss what effect, if any, community development activities

---

outside of the assessment area(s) and the broader statewide or regional area(s) that includes the institution's assessment area(s) may have on the rating. Charts and tables should be used whenever possible to summarize and effectively present the most critical or informative data used by the examiner in analyzing the institution's performance and reaching conclusions.

Write a paragraph about the institution's record of complying with the antidiscrimination laws (ECOA, FHA, or HMDA) using the following guidelines:

- When substantive violations involving illegal discrimination or discouragement are found by the OCC or identified through self-assessment(s), state that substantive violations were found, whether they caused the CRA rating to be adjusted downward, and why the rating was or was not adjusted. Identify the law(s) and regulations(s) violated, the extent of the violation(s) (e.g., widespread, or limited to a particular state, office, division, or subsidiary) and characterize management's responsiveness in acting upon the violation(s). Determine whether the institution has policies, procedures, training programs, internal assessment efforts, or other practices in place to prevent discriminatory or other illegal credit practices.

- If no substantive violations were found, state that no violations of the substantive provisions of the antidiscrimination laws and regulations were identified. Even if discrimination has not been found, comments related to the institution's fair lending policies, procedures, training programs and internal assessment efforts may still be appropriate. If applicable, technical violations cited in the report of examination should be presented in general terms.

Multistate Metropolitan Area

CRA RATING FOR (Name of MULTISTATE METROPOLITAN AREA):

[Complete for each multistate metropolitan area where an institution has branches in two or more states within the multistate metropolitan area.]
Summarize the major factors supporting the institution's multistate metropolitan area rating. When illegal discrimination or discouragement has been identified and has affected the rating, the conclusion should include a statement that the rating was influenced by violations of the substantive provisions of the antidiscrimination laws. The conclusion should not mention any technical violations of the antidiscrimination laws.

DESCRIPTION OF INSTITUTIONS OPERATIONS IN (Name of MULTISTATE METROPOLITAN AREA):

Describe the institution's operations within the multistate metropolitan area, including a description of each of the assessment areas that it serves within the multistate metropolitan area. Indicate how many of these assessment areas were reviewed using the full examination procedures.

CONCLUSIONS WITH RESPECT TO COMMUNITY DEVELOPMENT TEST IN (Name of MULTISTATE METROPOLITAN AREA):

Discuss the institution's CRA performance within the multistate metropolitan area. The facts, data and analyses that were used to form a conclusion about the rating should be reflected in the narrative, including institution strengths and areas for improvement. The narrative should clearly demonstrate how the results of the community development test analysis, as well as the institution's record in assessment areas examined using the limited examination procedures (located in the multistate metropolitan area), factored into the rating. Support your conclusions with an analysis of facts and data from the assessment areas reviewed using the full examination procedures. In addition, include discussions of facts and data for assessment areas reviewed using the limited examination procedures when appropriate. Indicate whether the institution's performance in the assessment areas reviewed using the limited examination procedures is consistent with the institution's record in assessment areas reviewed using the full examination procedures in the multistate metropolitan area. Charts and tables should be used whenever possible to summarize and effectively present the most critical or informative data used by the examiner in analyzing the institution's performance and reaching conclusions.

State

CRA RATING FOR (Name of STATE):

[If the institution has branches in more than one state, complete this section for each state. Otherwise, complete the Metropolitan Statistical Area and Non-Metropolitan Statewide Area presentations only, as applicable.]

Summarize the major factors supporting the institution's state rating. When illegal discrimination or discouragement has been identified and has affected the rating, the conclusion should include a statement that the rating was influenced by violations of the substantive provisions of the antidiscrimination laws. The conclusion should not mention any technical violations of the antidiscrimination laws.

DESCRIPTION OF INSTITUTION'S OPERATIONS IN (Name of STATE):

Describe the institution's operations within the state and the assessment area(s) that it serves. Information that may be important includes: total statewide assets; asset/loan portfolio mix; primary business focus; branching network; any merger or acquisition activity; and a brief description of the assessment areas within the state.

CONCLUSIONS WITH RESPECT TO PERFORMANCE TESTS IN (Name of STATE):

Discuss the institution's CRA performance within the state. The facts, data and analyses that were used to form a conclusion about the rating should be reflected in the narrative, including institution strengths and areas for improvement. The narrative should clearly demonstrate how the analyses of the performance criteria factored into the rating. Charts and tables should be used whenever possible to summarize and effectively present the most critical or informative data used by the examiner in analyzing the institution's performance and reaching conclusions.

Metropolitan Areas

CONCLUSIONS WITH RESPECT TO PERFORMANCE TESTS IN (Name of METROPOLITAN AREA):

Discuss the institution's CRA performance within the metropolitan area, including a description of the assessment area(s) that it serves within the metropolitan area. The facts, data and analyses that were used to form a conclusion should be reflected in the narrative, including institution strengths and areas for improvement. The narrative should clearly demonstrate how the analyses of the performance criteria factored into the metropolitan area conclusion. Support your conclusions with an analysis of facts and data across geographies and demographic groups in the assessment areas reviewed using the examination procedures. Discuss any additional facts and data considered.

Additionally, discuss the institution's record in assessment areas examined using the limited examination procedures (located in a metropolitan area). Indicate whether the institution's performance in the assessment areas reviewed using the limited examination procedures is consistent with the institution's record in assessment areas reviewed using the full examination procedures in the metropolitan area. Support your conclusions with appropriate facts and data.

Charts and tables should be used whenever possible to summarize and effectively present the most critical or informative data used by the examiner in analyzing the institution's performance and reaching conclusions.

Non-metropolitan Statewide Areas

CONCLUSIONS WITH RESPECT TO PERFORMANCE TESTS IN (Name of NON-METROPOLITAN STATEWIDE AREA):

Discuss the institution's CRA performance within the non-metropolitan statewide area, including a description of the assessment area(s) that it serves within the non-metropolitan statewide area. The facts, data and analyses that were used to form a conclusion should be reflected in the narrative, including institution strengths and areas for improvement. The narrative should clearly demonstrate how the analyses of the performance criteria factored into the conclusion for the non-metropolitan statewide area.

Support your conclusions with an analysis of facts and data across geographies and demographic groups in the assessment areas reviewed using the examination procedures. Discuss any additional facts and data considered. Additionally, discuss the institution's record in assessment areas examined using the limited examination procedures (located in the non-metropolitan statewide area.) Indicate whether the institution's performance in the assessment areas reviewed using the limited examination procedures is consistent with the institution's record in assessment areas reviewed using the full examination procedures in the non-metropolitan statewide area. Support your conclusions with facts and data as appropriate.

Charts and tables should be used whenever possible to summarize and effectively present the most critical or informative data used by the examiner in analyzing the institution's performance and reaching conclusions.

Other Activities

If a wholesale or limited purpose institution has adequately addressed the needs of its assessment area(s), qualified investments, community development loans, or community development services that benefit areas outside of the institution's assessment area(s) and the broader statewide or regional area(s) that includes the institution''s assessment areas may be considered. If the activities considered were not sufficient to raise the rating of the institution from an overall satisfactory to an outstanding, this section need only contain a statement that other activities were considered but did not affect the overall rating of the institution.

Charts or tables may be useful in depicting information throughout the presentation.

SUMMARY OF INSTITUTION'S OTHER COMMUNITY DEVELOPMENT ACTIVITIES

Summarize the institution's community development activities outside its assessment area(s) and the broader statewide or regional area(s) that includes the institution's assessment area(s). Include number, volume, and types of community development loans, qualified investments, and community development services.

DISCUSSION OF PERFORMANCE IN OTHER COMMUNITY DEVELOPMENT ACTIVITIES

Summarize the institution's performance in other community development activities. The narrative should demonstrate how these activities influenced the overall rating for the institution.

Sample Appendix A – Scope of Examination

Write a short description of the scope of the examination. At a minimum, discuss the specific products reviewed, the names of (any) affiliates reviewed and their corresponding products, the institution's assessment areas and whether its activities in the assessment areas were reviewed using the examination procedures, and the time period covered in the review.

Charts and tables that illustrate the scope of the examination may be useful for large institutions with multiple assessment areas or institution's that use data from their affiliates. Tables such as the ones below may be used as a supplement to the discussion of the scope or in lieu thereof.

Sample Scope of Examination

Time period reviewed	1/1/95 to 6/30/96		
Financial Institution XYZ National Bank, Wilmington			**Products Reviewed** Community Development investments; community development services
Affiliate(s)	**Affiliate Relationship**		**Products Reviewed**
XYZ Corporation, Chicago	Bank Holding Company		Qualified Investments
XYZ Investment Corp, Chicago	Holding Co. Subsidiary		Qualified Investments
List of Assessment Areas and Type of Examination			
Assessment Area	**Type of Exam**	**Branches Visited**	**Other Information**
Delaware MSA 1111 Wilmington	On-site	Brandywine, Newark	None
South Dakota MSA 1234 Sioux Falls	Off-site	Indian Lake	Sioux Falls operations acquired in an acquisition dated 1/1/95 from ABC Corp. The scope only includes lending activity since that date.

Sample Appendix B – Summary of State and Multistate MSA Ratings

State or Multistate MSA Name	State or Multistate MSA Rating

Background and Purpose

These guidelines apply to any type of institution that is subject to the CRA and that wishes to request that it be evaluated on the basis of a strategic plan. These guidelines also apply to requests for approval to amend a strategic plan.

The strategic plan evaluation option in the regulation provides an institution with the opportunity to tailor its CRA objectives to the needs of its community and to its own capacities, business strategies and expertise. Not all of the factors described in the regulation, therefore, would necessarily apply to each strategic plan. An institution has a great deal of latitude in constructing a strategic plan, but it is expected that public participation in development of the plan will provide an institution access to the fullest possible information about the needs of its community and how those needs might be met.

The required contents of a strategic plan and the OCC's criteria for evaluating a strategic plan are specified in the OCC's CRA regulation, 12 CFR 25.27. These guidelines do not supplant the regulation; rather, they are intended to serve as guidance in the preparation of a strategic plan and submission of the plan to the OCC for approval. These guidelines specify the types of information that a national bank will generally need to submit in requesting that it be evaluated on the basis of a strategic plan. In addition to the items listed in the guidelines, a national bank may submit any other information that it may consider relevant to the OCC's decision.

Performance Context

A proposed strategic plan will be evaluated in the context of the information described generally in the OCC's CRA regulation, 12 CFR 25.21(b). This information could include, as appropriate: demographic data on median income and household income; housing costs; lending, investment and service opportunities in the institution's assessment area(s); the institution's product offerings and business strategy; institutional capacity and constraints (including the institution's size, financial condition, and economic climate); past performance of the institution; and relevant information from the institution's public file. The agencies will not expect the institution to supply more information regarding the performance context than it would normally develop to prepare a business plan or to identify potential customers, including low- and moderate-income individuals or geographies in its assessment area(s). Information submitted by the institution will be considered along with information from community, government, civic, and other sources.

Public Comments

Public comment is important to, but not determinative of, the decision on strategic plan approval. The public comments will be reviewed by the OCC to determine whether the national bank offered the opportunity for community input into the plan, to assess the degree of support for the institution's goals, and to evaluate the appropriateness of those goals. The agency will, if necessary, consider other information regarding the performance context in addition to the public comments and information submitted by the institution.

Alternative Assessment Method

A national bank may elect in its strategic plan, that if it fails to meet substantially the plan goals for a satisfactory rating, its CRA performance will be evaluated under the (1) lending, investment, and service tests (2) community development test or (3) small-institution performance standards, whichever may be appropriate. If such an election is not made in the strategic plan, the national bank will be evaluated only under the strategic plan, and failure to meet substantially the goals set forth for satisfactory performance will result in assignment of a rating of "needs to improve" or "substantial noncompliance."

Preparing and Submitting a Proposed Strategic Plan

An institution's proposed strategic plan, along with all requested information, should be submitted in writing to the federal regulatory agency that exercises primary supervisory authority with respect to that institution. If a proposed plan covers more than one affiliated institution, a copy of the entire plan should be submitted to each federal bank regulatory agency that has primary supervisory responsibility for one or more institutions covered by the plan. If a proposed strategic plan is being submitted on behalf of more than one institution, each institution must receive the approval of its own supervisory agency for those portions of the plan relating to that institution's CRA responsibilities.

A proposed strategic plan that covers one or more national banks should be submitted to the appropriate office designated by the OCC. For this purpose, the appropriate office shall be the Community and Consumer Policy Department. Inquiries concerning the preparation of a strategic plan should also be directed to that office at the following address: Deputy Comptroller for Community and Consumer Policy, Office of the Comptroller of the Currency, Attn: CRA Strategic Plan, Washington, DC 20219.

The OCC may require the national bank to submit any additional statements or information that it deems necessary. It is the institution's responsibility to submit the information necessary to demonstrate that the proposed strategic plan meets the criteria for approval.

Each request for approval of a proposed strategic plan should name a contact person at the national bank. Strategic plans that include more than one national bank affiliate may designate a single contact person for all the covered institutions; or separate contacts for one or more of the national bank affiliates. Upon receipt, the Community and Consumer Policy Department will review the proposed strategic plan and related material to determine if the request is complete. A request for approval of a strategic plan will be deemed to be complete when all relevant information identified in these guidelines has been received by the OCC. If the request is deemed to be incomplete, the OCC will notify the requesting institution(s) and a request for additional information will be sent to the named contact person. If any information initially furnished with the request changes significantly during the processing of that request, the national bank should communicate those changes promptly to the Community and Consumer Policy Department.

Each request for approval of a proposed strategic plan should also contain a proposed effective date. The proposed effective date should be at least 90 days after the request is submitted to the OCC. The national bank will not be evaluated under a strategic plan until the institution has been operating under an approved and effective plan for at least one year.

OCC Notification of Decision

The OCC will act upon a national bank's request for approval of its proposed strategic plan within 60 calendar days after the agency receives the complete plan, unless the agency extends the review period for good cause. The OCC will notify the institution of any extension of the review period, the reason for the extension and the date by which the agency expects to act upon the request. If the OCC fails to act within this time period, the proposed plan will be deemed approved.

If a strategic plan covering multiple institutions must be approved by more than one regulatory agency, each agency will issue a decision approving or denying the request with respect to the institution(s) for which that agency has primary supervisory responsibility.

Confidentiality

Under the provisions of the Freedom of Information Act (FOIA), 5 U.S.C. 552, a request for approval of a proposed strategic plan that is submitted to the OCC is a public document and is available to the public upon request. The OCC's decision approving or denying a proposed strategic plan may also be available to the public under the FOIA.

A national bank may request confidential treatment for information that would be exempt from public disclosure under the FOIA. For example, if the requesting national bank is of the opinion that disclosure of commercial or financial information would likely result in substantial harm to its competitive position or that of its affiliates, or that disclosure of information of a personal nature would result in a clearly unwarranted invasion of personal privacy, confidential treatment of such information may be requested. This request for confidential treatment must be submitted in writing concurrently with the filing of the strategic plan and must discuss in detail the justification for confidential treatment. Justification must be provided for each item or category of information for which confidential treatment is requested. The institution's request for confidentiality should explain the harm that would result from public release of the information.

Information for which confidential treatment is sought should be: (1) segregated from the other information that is submitted; (2) specifically identified in the nonconfidential portion of the strategic plan (by reference to the confidential section), and; (3) labeled "Confidential." The requesting national bank should follow this same procedure on confidentiality with regard to filing any supplemental information. The OCC will determine whether information labeled "Confidential" will be so regarded, and will advise the requesting national bank of any decision to make information labeled "Confidential" available to the public.

A national bank should follow the rules stated above when submitting confidential supervisory information, which includes any information contained in, related to, or derived from reports of examination and inspection, or confidential operating and condition reports.

Requested Information

The requirements for a strategic plan are contained in the OCC's CRA regulation, 12 CFR 25.27. A national bank requesting approval for a strategic plan will generally need to submit:

* The names of each institution joining in the plan and a description of how they are affiliated. The agencies will approve a joint plan only if the plan

---

provides measurable goals for each institution for each assessment area covered by the plan.

- For each institution, an identification of the assessment area(s) covered by the plan, including a list of the geographies involved.

- The proposed term of the plan. A plan may have a term of no more than five years.

- The proposed effective date for the plan, which should be at least 90 days after the plan is submitted to the OCC.

- A description of the formal or informal public input received during development of the plan. Copies of any written comments that were received during the development of the plan that was released for public comment may be provided.

- A copy of the required public notice and the name(s) of the newspaper(s) in which the required notice was published.

- Copies of all written comments received during the comment period.

- A copy of the strategic plan released for public comment, if it is different from the strategic plan being submitted for agency approval.

- For each assessment area for each institution covered by the plan, copies of any information developed in the institution's normal business planning that it wants the agency to consider regarding lending, investment, and service opportunities in the assessment area, including a description of any legal constraints or limitations that affect the type of loans, investments or services that the institution may make or offer.

- For each assessment area for each institution covered by the plan, measurable goals for helping to meet the credit needs of the assessment area, particularly the needs of low- and moderate-income geographies and individuals. If the plan for an institution encompasses the activities of **nondepository institution affiliates**, it is not necessary to state separate goals for each such affiliate.

Generally, a national bank shall discuss its plans regarding lending, investments, and services with an emphasis on lending and lending-related activities. The plan, however, need not specify measurable goals in all three categories. Generally, a national bank that has been designated a wholesale or limited-purpose institution shall emphasize community development lending, qualified investments, and community development services. A plan, however, need not follow the general rule if the emphasis of the plan is responsive to the characteristics and credit needs of the particular assessment area(s), considering the public comments and the institution's capacity, constraints, product offerings, and business strategy.

Accordingly, for each assessment area for each institution covered by the plan:

- A plan **must** include measurable annual goals that, if met, would constitute "satisfactory" performance. Multi-year plans must include annual interim measurable goals. Measurable goals are goals that are stated in quantifiable terms. Institutions, however, are provided flexibility in specifying goals. For example, an institution may provide ranges of lending amounts in different categories of loans. It would also be appropriate for an institution to plan on making a certain number of loans or lending a specific amount in a particular area or with respect to a particular project. An institution might plan on providing community services measured in terms of the frequency of use or amount of staff resources involved. In addition, an institution could provide a menu of activities, each with a weighted point value, from which a measurable goal could be stated in point totals. Measurable goals may also be linked to funding requirements of certain public programs or indexed to other external factors as long as these mechanisms provide a quantifiable standard.

- A plan **may** also include measurable goals for any institution covered by the plan that, if met, would constitute "outstanding" performance for that institution.

- An indication whether any institution covered by the plan elects to be evaluated under another assessment method (e.g., large retail institution assessment method) if the institution fails to meet substantially the strategic plan goals for a "satisfactory" performance rating.

Examination Scope

1. For institution's with more than one assessment area, select assessment areas for review. To select one or more assessment areas for an on-site examination, review previous performance evaluations, available community contact materials, reported lending data and demographic data on each assessment area and consider factors such as:

    a. The level of the institution's lending, investment and service activity in the different assessment areas, particularly in low- and moderate-income areas.

    b. The number of other institutions in the different assessment areas and the importance of the institution under examination in meeting credit needs in the different assessment areas, particularly in areas with a limited number of financial service providers.

    c. The existence of apparent anomalies in the reported lending data for any particular assessment area(s).

    d. The time since the assessment area(s) was most recently examined on-site.

    e. Performance that falls short of plan goals based on a review of available data.

    f   The institution's previous CRA performance in the different assessment areas.

    g. Comments from the public regarding the institution's CRA performance.

2. For interstate institutions, a rating must be assigned for each state in which the institution has a branch and in every multistate MSA where the institution has branches in two or more of the states that comprise that multistate MSA. Select one or more assessment areas in each state for examination using these procedures.

Performance Context

1. Review the institution's public file for any comments received by the institution or the agency since the last CRA performance evaluation that assists in evaluating the institution's record of meeting plan goals.

2. Consider any information that the institution provides on its record of meeting plan goals.

3. Review community contact forms prepared by the regulatory agencies and consult with district community reinvestment and development specialists to obtain information that will assist in the evaluation of the bank. Contact local community, governmental, or economic development representatives to update or supplement information about the institution's record of meeting plan goals.

4. As necessary, consider any information the institution or others may provide on local community and economic conditions that may affect the institution's ability to meet plan goals or otherwise assist in the evaluation of the institution.

Performance Criteria

1. Review the following:

   a. The approved plan and approved amendments.

   b. The agency's approval process files.

   c. Written comments from the public that the institution or the agency received since the plan became effective.

2. Determine whether the institution achieved its performance goals for each assessment area examined by:

   a. Reviewing the plan's measurable annual goals for each performance category and assessment area(s) to be reviewed.

   b. Obtaining information and data about the institution's actual performance for the period that has elapsed since the previous examination.

   c. Comparing the plan goals for each assessment area reviewed to the institution's actual performance since its last examination in each assessment area reviewed to determine if all of the plan's goals have been met.

3. If any goals were not met, form a conclusion as to whether the plan goals were "substantially met." In doing so, consider the number of unmet goals, the degree to which the goals were not met, the importance of those goals to the plan as a whole, and the reasons why the goals were not met (e.g., economic factors beyond the institution's control) .

4. Discuss with management the preliminary findings.

5. Summarize conclusions about the institution's performance.

Ratings

These instructions assume that the strategic plan covers all of the institution's assessment areas. If not, the analysis of performance for the assessment area(s) covered by the strategic plan must be combined with the analyses for assessment areas that were subject to other assessment method(s) in order to assign a rating.

1. Group the analyses of the assessment areas examined by MSA and non-MSA areas within each state where the institution has branches. If an institution has branches in two or more states of a multistate MSA, group the assessment areas that are in that MSA.

2. If the institution has substantially met its plan goals for a satisfactory rating or, if applicable, an outstanding rating, in all assessment areas reviewed, summarize conclusions about the institution's performance in each MSA and the non-MSA area of each state in which an assessment area was examined using these procedures. Assign the appropriate preliminary rating for the institution and, as applicable, each state or multistate MSA and proceed to step 6, below.

3. If the institution did not substantially meet its plan goals in each assessment area, check to determine if the institution elected in its plan to be evaluated under an alternate assessment method.

   a. If the institution did not elect in the plan to be evaluated under an alternate assessment method, assign to those assessment areas in which plan goals were not substantially met a rating of "needs to improve" or "substantial noncompliance" depending on the number of goals missed, the extent to which they were missed, and their importance to the plan overall.

   b. If the institution elected in its plan to be evaluated under an alternate assessment method, perform the appropriate procedures to evaluate and rate the institution's performance in those assessment areas in which the institution did not meet plan goals.

4. For institutions operating in multiple assessment areas, determine the relative importance of the assessment areas reviewed in forming conclusions for each MSA and the non-MSA area within each state and for any multistate MSA where the institution has branches in two or more states. In making that determination, consider:

    a. The significance of the institution's activities in each compared with the institution's overall activities.

    b. The lending, service, and investment opportunities in each.

    c. The significance of the institution's loans, qualified investments, and lending-related services, as applicable, for each, particularly in light of the number of other institutions and the extent of their activities in each.

    d. Demographic and economic conditions in each.

5. For an institution operating in multiple MSAs or non-MSA areas in one or more states or multistate MSAs, assign a preliminary rating for each state and multistate MSA. To determine the relative significance of each MSA and non-MSA area to the rating in a state, consider:

    a. The significance of the institution's activities in each compared with the institution's overall activities.

    b. The lending, service, and investment opportunities in each.

    c. The significance of the institution's loans, qualified investments, and lending-related services, as applicable, for each, particularly in light of the number of other institutions and the extent of their activities in each.

    d. Demographic and economic conditions in each.

6. For institutions with operations in more than one state, assign a preliminary overall rating. When determining the relative significance of the institution's performance in each state or multistate MSA to its overall rating consider:

    a. The significance of the institution's activities in each compared with the institution's overall activities.

    b. The lending, service, and investment opportunities in each.

c. The significance of the institution's loans, qualified investments, and lending-related services, as applicable, for each, particularly in light of the number of other institutions and the extent of their activities in each.

d. Demographic and economic conditions in each.

7. Review the results of the fair lending component of the most recent compliance examination. To determine whether evidence of discrimination should lower the institution's overall CRA rating or, if applicable, any of its state or multistate MSA ratings, consider the following:

a. The nature and extent of the evidence.

b. The policies and procedures that the institution has in place to prevent discrimination or other illegal credit practices.

c. Any corrective action the institution took, or committed to take, particularly voluntary corrective action resulting from a self-assessment conducted before the examination.

d Other relevant information, such as the institution's past fair lending performance.

8. Discuss conclusions with management and assign a final rating to the institution and state or multistate MSA ratings, as applicable.

9. Write comments for the public evaluation and the examination report.

Public File Checklist

1. There is no need to review each branch or each complete public file during every examination. When determining the extent to which the institution's public files should be reviewed, consider the institution's record of compliance with the public file requirements in previous examinations, its branching structure and changes to it since its last examination, complaints about the institution's compliance with the public file requirements, and any other relevant information.

2. In any review of the public file undertaken, determine, as needed, whether branches display an accurate public notice in their lobbies; a complete public file is available in the institution's main office and at least one branch in each state, and the public file available in the main office and in a branch in each state contains:

a. A copy of the approved strategic plan.

b. All written comments from the public relating to the institution's CRA performance and any responses to them for the current and preceding two calendar years (except those that reflect adversely on the good name or reputation of any persons other than the institution).

c. The institution's most recent CRA performance evaluation.

d. A map of each assessment area showing its boundaries and, on the map or in a separate list, the geographies contained within the assessment area.

e. A list of the institution's branches, branches opened and closed during the current and each of the two previous calendar years, their street addresses and geographies.

f. A list of services (loan and deposit products and transaction fees) generally offered, and hours of operation at the institution's branches, including a description of any material differences in the availability or cost of services between those locations.

g. The institution's CRA disclosure statement(s) for the two previous calendar years.

h. A quarterly updated progress report of the institution's efforts to improve its record if it received a less than satisfactory rating during its most recent CRA examination.

I. HMDA disclosure statements for the two previous calendar years and those of each nondepository affiliate the institution has elected to include in assessment of its CRA record, if applicable.

j. The number and amount of consumer loans, for large banks, if applicable.

k. The loan-to-deposit ratio, for small institutions.

3. In any branch review undertaken, determine whether the branch provides the most recent public evaluation and a list of services available at the branch or a description of material differences from the services generally available at the institution's other branches.

Public Disclosure

(Date of Evaluation)**

Community Reinvestment Act
Performance Evaluation

Name of Depository Institution
Institution's Identification Number

Mailing Address of Institution

Name of Supervisory Agency

Address of Supervisory Office

NOTE: **This evaluation is not, nor should it be construed as, an assessment of the financial condition of this institution. The rating assigned to this institution does not represent an analysis, conclusion or opinion of the federal financial supervisory agency concerning the safety and soundness of this financial institution.**

* This is a sample created for a large, multistate institution, and should be adjusted, as appropriate, to reflect the scope of the institution's operations. Refer to the "Instructions for Writing Public Evaluations" in this booklet for further guidance.

** Use the start date of the onsite examination reported in the type 02 or type 99 analysis that supports the CRA rating.

General Information

The Community Reinvestment Act (CRA) requires each federal financial supervisory agency to use its authority when examining financial institutions subject to its supervision, to assess the institution's record of meeting the credit needs of its entire community, including low- and moderate-income neighborhoods, consistent with safe and sound operation of the institution. Upon conclusion of such examination, the agency must prepare a written evaluation of the institution's record of meeting the credit needs of its community.

This document is an evaluation of the CRA performance of **(name of depository institution)** prepared by **(name of agency)**, the institution's supervisory agency, as of **(date of examination)**. The agency evaluates performance in assessment area(s), as they are delineated by the institution, rather than individual branches. This assessment area evaluation may include the visits to some, but not necessarily all of the institution's branches. The agency rates the CRA performance of an institution consistent with the provisions set forth in appendix A to 12 CFR part 25.

This institution elected to be evaluated under the strategic plan option. The plan, approved by the agency, sets forth goals for a "satisfactory"(and an "outstanding", if applicable) performance.

Institution's CRA Rating: This institution is rated _____.

Summarize the major factors supporting the institution's rating. When illegal discrimination or discouragement has been identified and has affected the rating, the summary should include a statement that the rating was influenced by violations of the substantive provisions of the antidiscrimination laws. The summary should not mention any technical violations of the antidiscrimination laws.

Conclusions

Summarize the facts, data, and analyses that were used to determine the overall rating, based on the institution's plan goals and actual performance under the plan. The discussion should be organized broadly around the lending, investment, and service goals, as applicable. If the institution has not substantially met its goals, discuss the effect, if any, changed circumstances may have on the rating. Charts and tables should be used whenever possible to summarize and effectively present the most critical or informative data used by the examiner in analyzing the institution's performance and reaching conclusions.

Write a paragraph about the institution's record of complying with the antidiscrimination laws (ECOA, FHA, or HMDA) using the following guidelines:

- When substantive violations involving illegal discrimination or discouragement are found by the OCC or identified through self-assessment(s), state that substantive violations were found, whether they caused the CRA rating to be adjusted downward, and why the rating was or was not adjusted. Identify the law(s) and regulations(s) violated, the extent of the violation(s) (e.g., widespread, or limited to a particular state, office, division, or subsidiary) and characterize management's responsiveness in acting upon the violation(s). Determine whether the institution has policies, procedures, training programs, internal assessment efforts, or other practices in place to prevent discriminatory or other illegal credit practices.

- If no substantive violations were found, state that no violations of the substantive provisions of the antidiscrimination laws and regulations were identified. Even if discrimination has not been found, comments related to the institution's fair lending policies, procedures, training programs and internal assessment efforts may still be appropriate. If applicable, technical violations cited in the report of examination should be presented in general terms.

Multistate Metropolitan Area

CRA RATING FOR (Name of MULTISTATE METROPOLITAN AREA):

[Complete for each multistate metropolitan area where an institution has branches in two or more states within the multistate metropolitan area.]

Summarize the major factors supporting the institution's multistate metropolitan area rating.

When illegal discrimination or discouragement has been identified and has affected the rating, the conclusion should include a statement that the rating was influenced by violations of the substantive provisions of the antidiscrimination laws. The conclusion should not mention any technical violations of the antidiscrimination laws.

CONCLUSIONS WITH RESPECT TO PERFORMANCE IN (Name of MULTISTATE METROPOLITAN AREA):

Discuss the institution's CRA performance within the multistate metropolitan area. The facts, data and analyses that were used to form a conclusion about the rating, as well as the institution's record in assessment areas in the multistate metropolitan area that were examined using the limited examination procedures, should be reflected in the narrative. The discussion should be based on the institution's plan goals and actual performance under the plan, and organized around the lending, investment and service goals, as applicable. If the institution has not substantially met its goals, discuss the effect, if any, changed circumstances may have on the rating. Charts and tables should be used whenever possible to summarize and effectively present the most critical or informative data used by the examiner in analyzing the institution's performance and reaching conclusions.

If the institution's assessment area(s) are smaller than the boundaries of the multistate metropolitan area, a discussion of the assessment areas examined should be included. Refer to the assessment area discussion, below.

State

CRA RATING FOR (Name of STATE):

[If the institution has branches in more than one state, complete this section for each state. Otherwise, complete the Metropolitan Area and Non-Metropolitan Statewide Area presentations only, as applicable.]

Summarize the major factors supporting the institution's state rating. When illegal discrimination or discouragement has been identified and has affected the rating, the conclusion should include a statement that the rating was influenced by violations of the substantive provisions of the antidiscrimination laws. The conclusion should not mention any technical violations of the antidiscrimination laws.

CONCLUSIONS WITH RESPECT TO PERFORMANCE IN (Name of STATE):

Discuss the institution's CRA performance within the state. The facts, data and analyses that were used to form a conclusion about the rating, based on the institution's plan goals and actual performance under the plan, should be reflected in the narrative. The discussion should be organized around the lending, investment and service goals, as applicable. If the institution has not substantially met its goals, discuss the effect, if any, changed circumstances may have on the rating. Charts and tables should be used whenever possible to summarize and effectively present the most critical or informative data used by the examiner in analyzing the institution's performance and reaching conclusions.

Metropolitan Areas

CONCLUSIONS WITH RESPECT TO PERFORMANCE IN (Name of METROPOLITAN AREA AND STATE):

Discuss the institution's CRA performance within the metropolitan area. The facts, data and analyses that were used to form a conclusion, as well as the institution's record in assessment areas in the metropolitan areas that were examined using the limited examination procedures, should be reflected in the narrative. The discussion should be based on the institution's plan goals and actual performance under the plan, and organized around the lending, investment and service goals, as applicable. If the institution has not substantially met its goals, discuss the effect, if any, changed circumstances may have on the rating. Charts and tables should be used whenever possible to summarize and effectively present the most critical or informative data used by the examiner in analyzing the institution's performance and reaching conclusions.

If the institutions assessment area(s) are smaller than the boundaries of the metropolitan area, a discussion of the assessment areas examined should be included. Refer to the assessment area discussion, below.

Non-metropolitan Statewide Areas

CONCLUSIONS WITH RESPECT TO PERFORMANCE TESTS IN (Name of NON-METROPOLITAN STATEWIDE AREA):

Discuss the institution's CRA performance within the non-metropolitan statewide area. The facts, data and analyses that were used to form a conclusion, as well as the institution's record in assessment areas in the non-metropolitan statewide area that were examined using the limited examination procedures, should be reflected in the narrative. The discussion should be based on the institution's plan goals and actual performance under the plan, and organized around the lending, investment and service goals, as applicable. If the institution has not substantially met its goals, discuss the effect, if any, changed circumstances may have on the rating. Charts and tables should be used whenever possible to summarize and effectively present the most critical or informative data used by the examiner in analyzing the institution's performance and reaching conclusions.

A discussion of the assessment areas examined using the full examination procedures should be included. Refer to the assessment area discussion, below.

Assessment Area

This section applies to each assessment area examined using the examination procedures. Charts or tables may be useful in depicting information throughout the assessment area presentation.

Discussion of Performance in (Assessment Area Name)

Summarize the facts, data, and analyses that were used to form a conclusion on the institution's performance in the assessment area. This should compare and contrast the institution's plan goals for the assessment area and actual performance under the plan. Explain variances between the plan and actual results. If the institution has not substantially met its goals, discuss the performance context and its impact on the conclusion. The discussion should be organized around the lending, investment and service goals, as applicable. Use the chart below to supplement the written summary, and note whether the analysis was conducted on-site. (Repeat discussion for each assessment area.)

Sample Strategic Plan Goals and Actual Performance for Eden Prairie and Davis Counties in Minnesota to Obtain Satisfactory Rating

Strategic Plan Goal	Actual Performance
1. $1.5 million in small farm loans	1. $1.32 million in loans
2. $2.0 million in loans to small businesses	2. $3.7 million in loans
3. $500,000 in loans to start-up businesses	3. $390,000 in loans
4. Provide construction or permanent financing for 24-unit housing project for low-income elderly persons	4. Construction line of credit approved for $960,000. $100,000 disbursed to date.

Assessment Area (or Area Reviewed)

This section applies to assessment areas in which an examination was not conducted using the examination procedures. Multiple assessment areas within the same multistate MSA, MSA, or nonmetropolitan statewide area and not examined on-site, may be combined into one presentation. Charts or tables may be useful in depicting information throughout the presentation.

Discussion of Performance in (Name of Assessment Area/Area Reviewed)

Summarize the facts and data that were reviewed and indicate whether the institution's performance in the area reviewed is consistent with the institution's record in the multistate MSA, MSA, or nonmetropolitan statewide area.

Sample Appendix A – Scope of Examination

Write a short description of the scope of the examination. At a minimum, discuss the specific products reviewed, the names of (any) affiliates reviewed and their corresponding products, the institution's assessment areas and whether its activities in the assessment areas were reviewed using the examination procedures, and the time period covered in the review.

Charts and tables that illustrate the scope of the examination may be useful for large institutions with multiple assessment areas or institution's that use data from their affiliates. Charts, such as the ones below, may be used as a supplement to the discussion of the scope or in lieu thereof. (Note: Example provided for clarity.)

Sample Scope of Examination

Time Period Reviewed			1/1/95 to 6/30/96
Financial institution XYZ National Bank, Eden Prairie, MN			**Products reviewed** Small business and small farm loans
Affiliate(s)	**Affiliate relationship**		**Products reviewed**
XYZ Bancorp, Blue Earth, MN	Holding company		Investments
XYZ Community Development Corp., Blue Earth, MN	Holding Co. Subsidiary		Investments
XYZ Savings Bank, Blue Earth, MN	Thrift holding company subsidiary		Mortgage lending
XYZ National Bank, Tampa, FL	Holding company subsidiary		Credit cards
List of Assessment Areas and Type of Examination			
Assessment Area	**Type of Exam**	**Branches Visited**	**Other Information**
Minnesota--Davis County and Eden Prairie County (contiguous counties)	On-site		
Florida--City of Tampa	Off-site		

Sample Appendix B – Summary of State and Multistate MSA Ratings

State or Multistate MSA Name	State or Multistate MSA Rating

Cover Letter

Comptroller of the Currency
Administrator of National Banks

Duty Station
Street Address
City, State, ZIP Code
(Date)

Name of CEO
President & Chief Executive Officer
Name of Bank
Street & P. O. Box Number
City, State, ZIP Code

Dear Mr./Ms. (Name of Chief Executive Officer):

We will arrive at the bank on (**date**) to conduct an examination. Our objective is to evaluate the bank's record of performance in helping to meet the credit needs of your entire community as required by the Community Reinvestment Act (CRA). In order for us to effectively prepare for this examination, please provide the information listed in the attachment to this request letter.

Please send the information to the address reflected above as detailed on the enclosed list or be prepared to make it available upon our arrival. All information should be as of (**examination as of date**) unless otherwise indicated. Please send the requested items no later than (**examiner determined date**).

Should you have any questions, contact the undersigned at (**area code and telephone number**) or the (**city name**) Field Office at (**area code and telephone number**).

Sincerely,

– Signature –

(Name of Examiner)
National Bank Examiner

Enclosure

Exhibit – Sample Large Bank Request Letter Enclosure

The information should be as of (**examination as of date**), unless otherwise indicated.

Please **provide copies** of the following by (**date**) to national bank examiner (**name of examiner**) at (**mailing address**):   .

1. Data required to be maintained regarding small business and small farm loans, according to 12 CFR 25.42, for the current year.

2. The year-to-date HMDA loan application register, if applicable.

3. Any data collected on consumer loans, according to 12 CFR 25.42(c), that the bank wants considered.

4. Any internal geographic distribution analysis the bank wants considered.

5. Any internal loan distribution data by borrower income the bank wants considered.

6. A description of any innovative or flexible loan products including the number and aggregate dollar amount of such loans granted since the last examination.

7. A list of qualified community development (CD) loans and investments, by the bank or an affiliate, allocated by assessment area. Please see the attached instructions and be sure to include the following:

    CD Loans: Originations, purchases, unfunded commitments, letters of credit, loans by consortiums, and third-party loans granted   since the last examination.

    Qualified Investments: Investments that were sold or matured since the previous examination and those made before the previous examination that are still outstanding.

    Other Qualified   Qualifying grants, donations, or in-kind
    Investments: contributions of property made since the last examination.

8. A description of any innovative or complex investments made since the last examination.

---

9. Any information on alternative delivery systems and community development services not included in the public file that the bank wants considered.

Please make the following information available at the beginning of the examination (copies of documents are acceptable):

10. The CRA public file, including the two previous Home Mortgage Disclosure Act (HMDA) statements, if applicable.

11. The two previous CRA disclosure statements.

12. Any other information on the bank's lending capacity and the assessment area the bank wants considered in the evaluation of its performance.

13. A balance sheet as of the examination date and a copy of the most recent call report.

14. Any annual reports issued since the last examination.

15. The files for the qualified investments and loans that are listed in #7 above.

Exhibit – Sample Large Bank Wholesale/Limited-Purpose Request Letter Enclosure

The information should be as of (**examination as of date**) unless otherwise indicated.

Please **provide copies** of the following by (**date**) to national bank examiner (**name of examiner**) at (**mailing address**).

1. The year-to-date HMDA-loan application register (LAR).

2. Data required to be maintained regarding small business and small farm loans, according to 12 CFR 25.42, for the current year.

3. Any data collected on consumer loans, according to 12 CFR 25.42(c), that the bank wants considered.

4. Any internal geographic distribution analysis the bank wants considered.

5. Any internal loan distribution data by borrower income the bank wants considered.

6. A list of qualified community development loans and investments by the bank or an affiliate, allocated by assessment area. Please see the attached instructions and be sure to include the following:

CD Loans:	Originations, purchases, unfunded commitments, letters of credit, loans by consortiums, and third-party loans granted since the last examination.
Qualified Investments:	Investments that were sold or matured since the previous examination and those made before the previous examination that are still outstanding.
Other Qualified Investments:	Qualifying grants, donations, or in-kind contributions of property made since the last examination.

7. Information on the use of innovative or complex qualified investments, community development loans, and community development services.

8. A list of community development services by description and amount.

9. Any information on the community development services of an affiliate that the bank wants considered, provided the services are not claimed by another institution.

10. Any information on the lending capacity and assessment area the bank wants considered.

Please make the following information available at the beginning of the examination (copies of documents are acceptable):

11. The CRA public file, including the two previous Home Mortgage Disclosure Act (HMDA) Statements.

12. The two previous CRA disclosure statements.

13. Balance sheet for the examination date and a copy of the most recent call report.

14. Any annual reports issued since the last examination.

15. The files for the qualified investments and loans listed in #6 above.

Exhibit – Sample Large Bank Strategic Plan Request Letter Enclosure

The information should be as of **(examination as of date)**, unless otherwise indicated.

Please **provide copies** of the following by **(date)** to national bank examiner **(name of examiner)** at **(mailing address)**. .

1. Data required to be maintained regarding small business and small farm loans, according to 12 CFR 25.42, for the current year.

2. The year-to-date HMDA-loan application register (LAR).

3. Any data collected on consumer loans, according to 12 CFR 25.42(c), that the bank wants considered.

4. Any other loan data the bank wants considered including loans by an affiliate, a consortium, or a third party.

5. Any internal geographic distribution analysis that the bank wants considered.

6. Any internal loan distribution data by borrower income the bank wants considered.

7. If community development investments and loans are part of the bank's strategic plan, you are encouraged to submit information regarding these activities, allocated by assessment area. Please see the attached instructions.

8. Any data or reports used to evaluate performance against the approved strategic plan.

9. Any other information the bank wants considered.

Please make the following information available at the beginning of the examination (copies of documents are acceptable):

10. The CRA public file, including Home Mortgage Disclosure Act (HMDA) statements.

11. The two previous CRA disclosure statements.

12. A balance sheet as of the examination date and a copy of the most recent call report.

13. Any annual reports issued since the last examination.

14 If you have submitted information on community development investments and loans in #7 above, please make those files available for our review.

Community Development Investments and Loans
Instructions and Code Sheet

Please use these instructions to submit information about qualified community development (CD) investments and loans. We are requesting that you use these instructions to facilitate our importing the data into a database program for analytical purposes. We have developed this information into a form in Lotus 5.0 and have included the spreadsheet layout specifications in these instructions. We encourage you to use a compatible spreadsheet or other type of program to provide this information. You may choose to provide the information in an alternative format. However, the same information or data elements are requested. If you have questions about these instructions, you should contact your examiner-in-charge.

NOTE: Each qualified investment or CD loan should be entered on a separate line. List only investments and loans that meet the definition of "community development," as described in 12 CFR 25.12, the interagency interpretive letters, or the interagency CRA questions and answers.

"Third-Party Activity": If you want us to consider CD activities by an affiliate, consortium, or other third party you will need to assign a different code number to them. Use a separate code for each individual affiliate, and use the code "999" for other third parties. This will allow us to consider the third party's activity in that assessment area along with your activity and to look at the sources of the activities separately. Please include a list that cross-references the codes to the names of the third parties.

"AA#" — Assessment Area #: Enter the number of the assessment area that benefits from the activity. <u>Use the number that you reported to the FRB when you last submitted your list of assessment areas.</u>

"Located Outside AA?": If the location of the organization that is involved in the activity is outside the assessment area, enter a "Y" here. If the organization is within the assessment area, leave this space blank. If the organization is outside your assessment areas, and the activity does not benefit any specific assessment area, enter a "Y" in this space and use a "0" (zero) for the AA# (this primarily applies to limited-purpose or wholesale institutions).

"Does it benefit > 1 AA?": Enter a "Y" if the investment or loan benefits more than one assessment area. Be sure to list the activity under both assessment areas, and approximate the amount of the activity that should be credited to each. Leave this space blank if the activity only benefits one assessment area.

Date Originated: The date the loan was made or purchased, or the date the investment was placed or purchased.

Name: A descriptive name of the investment or loan.

"$ Amount of Qual. Investment": The dollar amount of the qualified investment when it was placed or purchased.

"$ Amount of CD Loan": The dollar amount of the CD loan when it was originated or purchased. Include only the bank's pro-rata share if the bank is participating with other institutions.   Include the total amount of a line of credit, not just the amount that was funded upon origination.

"$ Amount of Contingent CD Loan": The dollar amount of any contingent or unfunded CD loan or letter of credit when it was approved or purchased. This does not include unfunded balances on loans reported in the previous entry above.

Purpose: Enter one of the following sets of codes (e.g., 1a) to describe how the activity meets the CD definition. Select only one alpha code that best describes the loan or investment.

1. Affordable housing (including multifamily rental housing) for low- or moderate-income individuals
   a. Involves low-income housing tax credits.
   b. Provides financing for a housing consortium, Community Development Corporation (CDC), or other third party that provides affordable housing.
   c. Finances a revolving affordable housing loan fund.
   d. Finances construction of affordable housing.
   e. Finances a non-profit developer of affordable housing.
   f. Represents an affordable housing bond.

g. Is not adequately described by any of the foregoing.

2. Community services targeted to low- or moderate-income individuals
   a. Finance organizations that provide educational, health, or social services to such individuals.
   b. Finance organizations that provide job training or day care services to such individuals.
   c. Finance construction of a community facility that serves such individuals.
   d. Are not adequately described by any of the foregoing.

3. Activities that promote economic development by financing businesses or farms that meet the size eligibility standards of the Small Business Administration or have gross annual revenues of $1 million or less
   a. Finance a Small Business Investment Company (SBIC) or similar venture capital intermediary.
   b. Finance a revolving loan fund used to finance small businesses.
   c. Finance an organization that provides assistance to small businesses, such as a small-business development center or a small-business incubator.
   d. Are not adequately described by any of the foregoing.

4. Activities that revitalize or stabilize low- or moderate-income geographies
   a. Represent a bond for community development projects.
   b. Finance intermediaries, such as a Community Development Financial Institution (CDFI), minority- and women-owned financial institution, low-income or community development credit union.
   c. Finance redevelopment of a central business district area that is a low- or moderate-income area.
   d. Finance a business that stabilizes a low- or moderate-income area or that will be a significant employer of low- and moderate-income individuals.
   e. Finance local, state, or tribal government for community development activities.
   f. Are not adequately described by any of the foregoing.

Housing Detail — "# Units": If the activity is for code 1 (affordable housing), enter the number of housing units in the project.

Housing Detail — "% LMI": If the activity is for code 1 (affordable housing), enter the percentage of the project that is reserved for, or used by, low- or moderate-income individuals.

"Innovative or Complex?": Enter a "C" if you consider the activity to be complex; enter an "I" if you consider the activity to be innovative; or enter "B" if you consider the activity to be both complex and innovative. If the activity has neither of these characteristics, leave this space blank.

Comments: Use this space to add any comments you believe are necessary to further describe the investment or loan.

File Layout Instructions

The following is a summary of the file layout used in the sample spreadsheet we have developed.

Affiliate Activity:	width 6, centered
AA#:	width 6, centered
Located outside AA:	width 6, centered
Does it benefit >1 AA:	width 6, centered
Date originated:	width 10, date format
Name:	width 30
$ Amount Investment:	width 8, no decimal
$ Amount. Loan:	width 8, no decimal
$ Amount Unfunded:	width 8, no decimal
Purpose:	width 6, centered
Housing detail — # units:	width 6
Housing detail — % LMI:	width 6, percentage format, no decimal
Type of Financing Structure:	width 8, centered
Innovative or complex:	width 8, centered
Comments:	width 30

NOTE: In our sample spreadsheet (next page), we included subtotals after all of the entries for an assessment area, and a grand total at the end. In the bank is a multi-state one, it might be appropriate to have a subtotal for each state and for each multi-state MSA.

CD INVESTMENTS AND LOANS

BANK _____ ABC BANK _____

Third Party Activity	AA #	Located Outside AA?	Does it Benefit >1 AA?	Date Originated	Name	$ Amount of Qual. Investment	$ Amount of CD Loan	$ Amount of Contingent CD Loan	Purpose	Housing # units	Detail % LMI	Innovative or Complex?	Comments
3	1			01/15/97	Magical Apartments	1,000			1A	300	75%	C	
	1			02/22/97	Zippy's Grocery		500		4D			B	
					Total - AA 1	1,000	500	0		300			
	2		Y	11/04/96	Greater Maryland SBIC	750			3A			I	
	2			09/03/96	Woodrow Wilson High School	50			2A				
	2			05/15/97	Heavenly Manor		150		1D	100	100%		
					Total - AA 2	800	150	0		100			
1	3			06/30/96	Frederick Area Habitat for Humanity			200	1	20	100%		
	3	Y	Y	11/04/96	Greater Maryland SBIC	750		200	3A	20			
					Total - AA 3	750	0	200		20			
					Grand Total for the Bank	2,550	650	200		420			

Community Reinvestment Act
Examination Procedures

Laws

    12 USC 2901   Community Reinvestment Act of 1977

Regulations

    12 CFR 25   Regulation on Community Reinvestment Act

OCC Issuances

    OCC 97-26   "Performance Context"

    OCC 97-42   "Interagency Questions and Answers on CRA"

    OCC 98-53   "Income level, median family income"

    AL 98-16   "Accuracy of CRA Data in Large Banks"